Heroin and Other Opioids
Poppies' Perilous Children

ILLICIT AND MISUSED DRUGS

Abusing Over-the-Counter Drugs:
Illicit Uses for Everyday Drugs

Addiction in America:
Society, Psychology, and Heredity

Addiction Treatment: Escaping the Trap

Alcohol Addiction: Not Worth the Buzz

Cocaine: The Rush to Destruction

Dual Diagnosis: Drug Addiction and Mental Illness

Ecstasy: Dangerous Euphoria

Hallucinogens: Unreal Visions

Heroin and Other Opioids:
Poppies' Perilous Children

Inhalants and Solvents: Sniffing Disaster

Marijuana: Mind-Altering Weed

Methamphetamine: Unsafe Speed

Natural and Everyday Drugs:
A False Sense of Security

Painkillers: Prescription Dependency

Recreational Ritalin: The Not-So-Smart Drug

Sedatives and Hypnotics: Deadly Downers

Steroids: Pumped Up and Dangerous

Tobacco: Through the Smoke Screen

ILLICIT AND MISUSED DRUGS

Heroin and Other Opioids

Poppies' Perilous Children

by E. J. Sanna

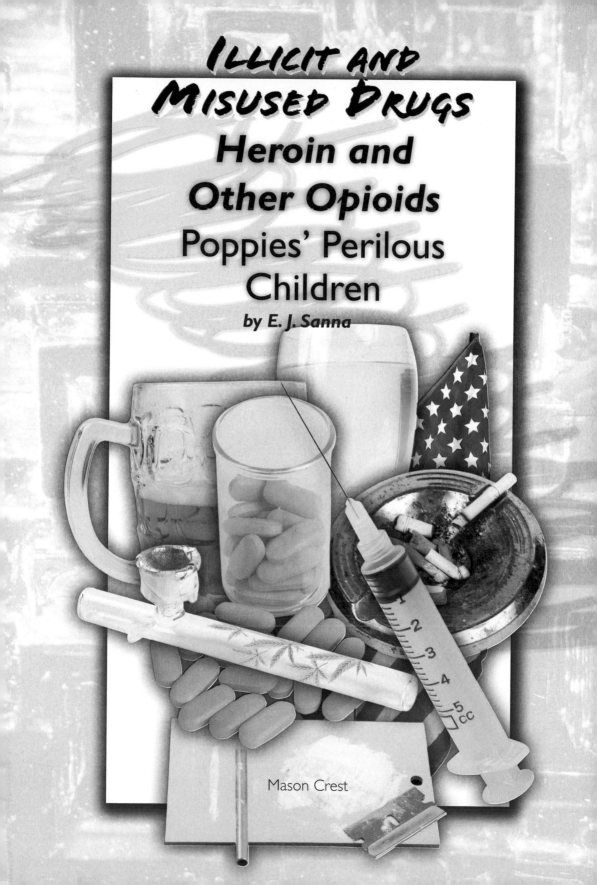

Mason Crest

Mason Crest
370 Reed Road
Broomall, Pennsylvania 19008
www.masoncrest.com

Printed in the Hashemite Kingdom of Jordan.

First printing
9 8 7 6 5 4 3 2 1

Library of Congress Cataloging-in-Publication Data

Sanna, E. J.
Heroin and other opioids : poppies' perilous children / E.J. Sanna.
    p. cm. — (Illicit and misused drugs)
Includes bibliographical references and index.
ISBN 978-1-4222-2433-5 (hardcover)
ISBN 978-1-4222-2452-6 (paperback)
ISBN 978-1-4222-2424-3 (series hardcover)
ISBN 978-1-4222-9297-6 (ebook)
1. Heroin—Juvenile literature. 2. Heroin abuse—Juvenile litera-ture. 3. Narcotics—Juvenile literature. I. Title.
  HV5822.H4S335 2012
  362.29'3—dc23
                                        2011032568

Interior design by Benjamin Stewart.
Cover design by Torque Advertising + Design.
Produced by Harding House Publishing Services, Inc.
www.hardinghousepages.com

CONTENTS

Introduction   6
1. What Are Opioids?   9
2. The History of Opioids   27
3. Who Uses Opioids?   51
4. The Dangers of Opioids   63
5. The Legal Consequences of Using
        Opioids   89
6. Treatment   105

Glossary   116
Further Reading   119
For More Information   120
Bibliography   121
Index   123
Picture Credits   127
Author/Consultant Biographies   128

INTRODUCTION

Addicting drugs are among the greatest challenges to health, well-being, and the sense of independence and freedom for which we all strive—and yet these drugs are present in the everyday lives of most people. Almost every home has alcohol or tobacco waiting to be used, and has medicine cabinets stocked with possibly outdated but still potentially deadly drugs. Almost everyone has a friend or loved one with an addiction-related problem. Almost everyone seems to have a solution neatly summarized by word or phrase: medicalization, legalization, criminalization, war-on-drugs.

For better and for worse, drug information seems to be everywhere, but what information sources can you trust? How do you separate misinformation (whether deliberate or born of ignorance and prejudice) from the facts? Are prescription drugs safer than "street" drugs? Is occasional drug use really harmful? Is cigarette smoking more addictive than heroin? Is marijuana safer than alcohol? Are the harms caused by drug use limited to the users? Can some people become addicted following just a few exposures? Is treatment or counseling just for those with serious addiction problems?

These are just a few of the many questions addressed in this series. It is an empowering series because it provides the information and perspectives that can help people come to their own opinions and find answers to the challenges posed by drugs in their own lives. The series also provides further resources for information and assistance, recognizing that no single source has all the answers. It should be of interest and relevance to areas of study spanning biology, chemistry, history, health, social studies and more. Its efforts to provide a real-world context for the information that is clearly presented but not overly simplified should be appreciated by students, teachers, and parents.

The series is especially commendable in that it does not pretend to pose easy answers or imply that all decisions can be made on the basis of simple facts: some challenges have no immediate or simple solutions, and some solutions will need to rely as much upon basic values as basic facts. Despite this, the series should help to at least provide a foundation of knowledge. In the end, it may help as much by pointing out where the solutions are not simple, obvious, or known to work. In fact, at many points, the reader is challenged to think for him- or herself by being asked what his or her opinion is.

A core concept of the series is to recognize that we will never have all the facts, and many of the decisions will never be easy. Hopefully, however, armed with information, perspective, and resources, readers will be better prepared for taking on the challenges posed by addictive drugs in everyday life.

— *Jack E. Henningfield, Ph.D.*

1 What Are Opioids?

Josh started snorting heroin when he was fourteen, mainly just because he was curious. When he was younger, he didn't really know what heroin was, and even when he tried it for the first time, all he knew was that it would make him high.

The first time he got high from heroin, he felt mellow and happy—and then he puked. Even that didn't feel so bad, though. Heroin gave him a special, magic sort of feeling; he had tried other drugs, but this was the best high he'd ever had—and he wanted more. He wasn't scared, because his friends who used heroin only described good things when they talked about the drug. They didn't tell Josh about the bad side.

Meanwhile, Josh also experimented with prescription drugs. He tried Percocet® the same year he first tried heroin. At a party, he saw a bunch of kids eating pills. "This

Prescription painkillers, such as Oxycontin and Percocet, are used sometimes as cheap alternatives to get high. Though prescribed by a doctor, these drugs are still dangerous when used incorrectly.

is way better than the high you get from pot," they told him. Josh wanted to see what it would feel like—and he liked it.

Eventually, Josh was eating pills whenever he was feeling sick from heroin or if he couldn't get heroin. After Percocet, he went on to use OxyContin®, Vicodin®, Ambien®, Coricidin®, and Unisom®. By now he knew that heroin could be dangerous, but he thought prescription drugs were safer. After all, why would doctors give them out if they weren't safe?

But Josh preferred heroin hands down. Some of his friends liked Oxy better than "dope," but OxyContin was too hard for Josh to get and it was harder to shoot it. He also had had a bad reaction to the Oxy. Still, Oxy gave him the same sort of high as heroin did. So he used Oxy when he couldn't get heroin, or if he was at a party where they were giving away Oxy free. And he'd buy the pills if someone was selling them cheaply enough. (Cheap in Josh's book was anywhere from $5 to $15 a pill.) Sometimes, he'd get lucky and his friends would hook him up with five pills for a dollar, and some kids who were stealing the pills from their parents' medicine cabinets would sell them for 25 cents a piece. Deals like that were just too good for Josh to pass up.

By now, most of Josh's friends used heroin, but a lot of them also used prescription drugs. His friends who had parents with prescription drugs would hand out whatever drugs they could get their hands on. Josh felt as though his friends were like his family. He was closer to them than he was to his siblings. They were always there for him. At least that's the way he felt when he was getting high.

Josh never thought about what was happening to his life. He never considered that he was turning into an addict. Most of the time, he was too high to care—and when he wasn't high, he spent all his time thinking about when and how he was going to get high the next time. He worried about how his next high would make him feel, whether it would be a good or bad high. That was his life: getting high and thinking about getting high.

Vaguely, he did realize that he could catch HIV/AIDS, since he was injecting heroin with needles that weren't always clean. But Josh didn't care. And he was lucky.

But when he got arrested for possessing a narcotic, he didn't feel so lucky. Inside prison, he resisted all treatment for a while, but toward the middle of his **mandated** time he started cooperating. For the first time in years, Josh wanted to be clean.

Inside his cell, Josh kept thinking about his dad. His father had given him so much, Josh realized, and now,

Josh wanted to give something back to him. Over the years, Josh's father had never given up on him. Sometimes, his dad got upset with him or frustrated and discouraged—but he would still visit Josh in prison and bring him things.

About this time, Josh also realized for the first time that he owed himself something, too: a better life, something more than just getting high all the time. He realized that in the old days, when all he did was get high, he had never had real friends. At the time, he had thought he did—but now he realized he hadn't.

Josh wished his life had gone differently; he wished he'd had friends who had told him he shouldn't use drugs, instead of encouraging him to try things that had led to addiction. And he wished he had been more honest with his father, that his dad realized he had a problem sooner than he did.

Kicking the habit was something Josh had to do for himself. It was the hardest thing he had ever done, though. He's still working on it, but he's certain now that it's what he wants for his life. Someday, he hopes to be a cook and build a good life for himself. He's looking forward to his future now.

Josh's story is a true one, adapted from his account on www.drugstory.org. His life is just one of many that have been damaged by opioids. These drugs have a long history; they have been used to make countless lives better; and they have also been the cause of countless addictions. Given how powerful these drugs are, it's ironic that their source is a pretty flower.

In the movie *The Wizard of Oz*, based on the book by L. Frank Baum, Dorothy and her friends find themselves passing through a poppy field on their way to the Emerald City. What they don't know is that this field was planted by the Wicked Witch of the West, who is hoping to steal the ruby slippers. Dorothy, Toto, and the Cowardly Lion fall asleep in the middle of the poppies, overcome by their scent. Fortunately, the Scarecrow and Tin Man are immune to the sedative power of the poppies, and they are able to rescue their friends and continue on their quest to find the wizard.

The Opium poppy (Papaver somniferum) is the source of natural opioids. The drugs are derived from the liquid found in the seedpod.

Heroin and Other Opioids—Poppies' Perilous Children

These tranquilizing bright red blossoms are actually opioids. While sniffing poppy flowers won't really make you lie down and fall asleep like it did in *The Wizard of Oz*, opioids were originally drugs derived from the poppy. For thousands of years, poppies have offered human beings a source of sleep, pain relief, and drowsy dreams.

Now, however, there are also **synthetic** opioids that, while made in the lab and not found naturally, share a common chemical structure with those found naturally. All opioids, both natural and synthetic, can be used to

Poppy seeds actually have some of the same chemicals that are found in the resin of the opium poppy. However, you would have to eat more than a normal amount of poppy seeds to have the chemicals show up on a drug test.

reduce pain. However, these drugs all have a high potential for abuse as well.

Heroin, Opium, Morphine, and Codeine: Natural Opioids

All the natural opioids are taken from a resin that is found in the seedpod of the Asian poppy. There are several different drugs that have been developed from this one single source, including heroin, opium, morphine, and codeine.

Heroin is the most commonly abused opioid. This is probably due to the fact that it is one of the fastest-acting opioid drugs; users can get a high faster than with most other opioids. The drug is developed from morphine, the largest chemical component of the poppy resin, and can be found as a brown or white powder.

There are many street names for heroin, including smack, H, junk, and skag. Black tar heroin is another kind of heroin, which is found mostly in the western or southwestern United States. This kind of heroin is produced in Mexico and is darker than the typical heroin, being anywhere from dark brown to black. Besides being characterized by its color, it is also sticky (like tar—therefore the name) or hard, unlike the powder form in which most heroin is sold.

The heroin that is sold on the street is rarely pure. Pure heroin is a bitter white powder; street heroin varies in color from the rarely available white of the pure drug to a dark brown. These differences in color are due not only to impurities that are introduced in the manufacturing process, but also to other drugs or substances that have been added to the heroin. Street heroin often contains sugar or *quinine* as well as the poppy derivative.

While the most efficient method of using heroin is to inject it, the drug can also be smoked or sniffed. In fact, as the fear of sharing needles and HIV/AIDS has grown, these alternative methods have become more popular than injecting.

Opium is another type of natural opioid. This dark brown drug is found in either large chunks or as a powder. It can be smoked or ingested. Opium was one of the first opioids discovered and has been used for centuries to cause a high. This is probably because it is one of the easiest opioids to make: simply open the unripened seedpod of the poppy and let the liquid in the pod harden. Today, opium is most popular in countries like Burma (Myanmar) and Afghanistan. Like all other opioids, it is highly addictive, and the user's body builds up a tolerance to the drug over time.

Morphine is used medically as a painkiller to treat severe or chronic pain. It is usually injected into the bloodstream, both in hospitals and by those who abuse the drug. However, morphine can also be found in tablet form. While it is often dissolved in a solution to allow for easy injection, the natural form of morphine is white, feathery crystals, called morphine sulfate.

Friedrich Wilhelm Adam Sertürner, a German pharmacist, discovered the drug in 1804. He named his new drug "morphium," after Morpheus, the Greek god of dreams. However, it was not until 1853 and the discovery of the hypodermic needle that morphine was used in any quantity. At this time, morphine became used not only as a pain reliever, but also as a cure for opium and alcohol addiction. Today, however, we know that morphine is just as addictive as either of these two drugs. In fact, after heroin, morphine is the most widely abused opioid.

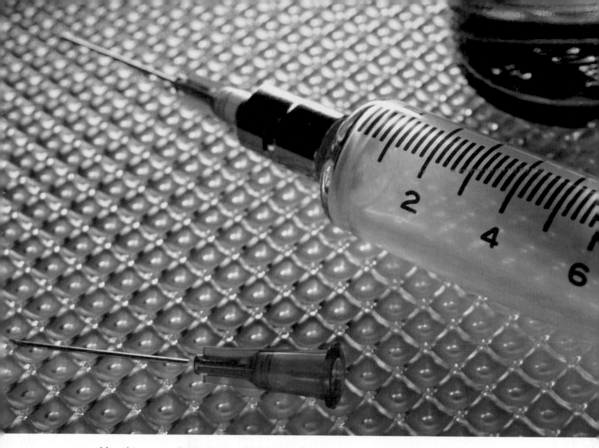

Morphine was discovered in 1804. However, it was not used extensively until after the invention of the hypodermic needle in the mid 1800s.

While morphine is not often found on the street like heroin and opium are, people still become addicted to the drug through prescriptions. When morphine is sold on the street, it can be referred to by such names as M, morph, or Miss Emma. Sometimes, dealers combine morphine with cocaine or methamphetamine. However, this is not a common combination and is rarely found on the street.

Codeine is the fourth naturally occurring opioid. It, like morphine, is used medically to relieve pain. However, codeine is not as strong as morphine and is used mostly to treat light to moderate pain. Most people have been prescribed this drug at some time or another, perhaps to

Opium is the most commonly abused opioid. It is also the easiest to make; just score the seed pod and let the white liquid dry to a brown resin.

relieve pain after surgery or other medical procedure. It is usually found in pill form, sometimes combined with other pain relievers like Tylenol®. However, codeine can also be used in a syrup. Many cough medicines contain a little codeine to help relax muscles and control coughing. Common forms of codeine can be found in the drugs Percodan®, Percocet, Tylox®, and oxycodone. There are no drugs that contain only codeine in the United States; however, Canada has a syrup called Paveral that contains only codeine.

While most codeine is either swallowed as a pill or in a syrup form, some users try to inject the drug directly into their bloodstreams. This can cause serious side effects like facial swelling, *pulmonary edema*, and even *seizures*.

While codeine is found naturally in the poppy plant and therefore is considered a natural opioid, it occurs in extremely small concentrations in raw opium—from 0.1 percent to 0.2 percent. Because of this, much of the codeine used for medical purposes is synthesized from morphine.

Synthetic Opioids

Synthetic opioids are similar to their natural counterparts in most ways. They are used for the same purposes; both natural and synthetic opioids can be used as painkillers. Both have a great potential for abuse and can be highly addictive. The only difference is that some are found naturally in the poppy flower while others are made in a lab. Some opioids, like hydrocodone, oxycodone, and meperidine, are only partly synthetic. They are made by combining a natural opioid with some other kind of drug. Others, however, are made solely in the laboratory. These synthetic drugs include methadone, propoxyphene, and fentanyl.

An Opioid High

Most opioid users take the drug for the immediate high they get when they ingest or inject whatever opioid they use. For example, many heroin users report feeling *euphoric* immediately after taking the drug. It is later that the physical effects of the drug become evident. However, there may be no physical effects at all except for relief from pain if the dosage is normal or if the user has developed a tolerance to the drug.

While the effects of all the opioids differ slightly, there are some general similarities. For example, opioids, sometimes referred to as narcotics, can often cause slowed reflexes and breathing, cold skin, and vomiting, as well as a general sedation. In this regard, they are similar to many other *sedatives*. Like other sedatives, they relax the user; however, right after ingestion (through whatever method) many users experience a rush. While this is the reason many people take the drug, effects can be

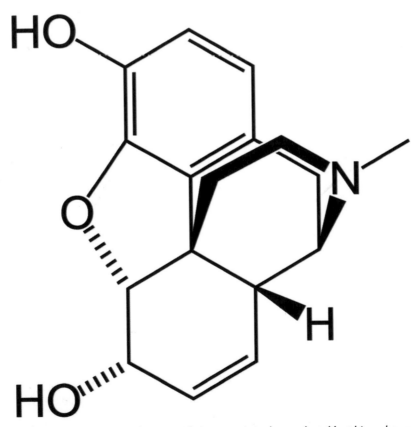

Opium is one of the weakest opioids because it is the crudest. Morphine, shown here, is one of the strongest because it is extracted from opium and purified.

paired with other, less desirable side effects such as rest-lessness, nausea, and/or vomiting. At other times, a user can go back and forth, from sleepy to wide-awake; this is referred to as being "on the nod."

Morphine, like other opioids, affects the central ner-vous system. This is how it relieves pain. However, this can also lead to other effects like the impairment of men-tal and physical capabilities and the **abatement** of anxi-ety and stress. Other common side effects include consti-pation and a decrease in appetite. Morphine can affect the reproductive organs as well; the drug reduces the sex drive and can disrupt women's menstrual cycles.

All opioids have similar effects on the body. The difference between them is in the strength of the drug. Opium is the weakest of the naturally found opioids, as it is the crudest form. Morphine, however, is one of the strongest.

Method of Action

How opioids affect the body depends on how they in-teract with the body's biological system. The chemical composition of these drugs is such that there is a "key" that imitates the body's natural **endorphins**. Because of this, they are able to attach to endorphin receptors in the brain, taking the place of the naturally occurring chemicals. Concentrations of these receptors are located in various parts of the brain, leading to the specific side effects that narcotics have on people.

The first area that has a concentration of these recep-tors is in the area of the brain that affects pain. When opioids join to the receptors here, they make pain feel less threatening or dangerous. This is how they work as painkillers; instead of removing the pain completely, they tell the body that the pain is meaningless and harmless, so the body ignores the feeling. Opioids are considered useful painkillers and are often prescribed by doctors not only for this reason but because there is no effect on other senses. Other painkillers, like ether, barbiturates, and even alcohol, can negatively affect motor coordination, control, and even make a patient lose consciousness if given in large enough doses. Opioids, on the other hand, can merely make a patient feel drowsy, and this only occurs at larger doses than are normally prescribed.

Opioids, also called narcotics, have similar effects to other sedatives. After an initial rush, opioids cause slowed breathing, cold skin, vomiting and general sedation.

Another concentration of endorphin receptors is found in the respiratory system. These are the cells that regulate the breathing rate according to the current situation (for example, the breathing rate speeds up during exercise and slows down when the body is at rest). When the opioids bond to these receptors, it causes both the rate of breathing and the depth of each individual breath to decrease. If a user takes too much, breathing can even stop, causing the person to die from a lack of oxygen.

The area of the brain that controls nausea also contains receptors. When opioids are introduced into the system, they cause the stomach muscles to contract, resulting in nausea and vomiting. For this reason, scientists have developed a synthetic opioid, apomorphine, which is used for just this purpose medically.

There are other clusters of receptors all over the body. In the digestive system, for instance, opioids can cure diarrhea by stopping intestinal *peristalsis*. In the *endocrine system*, opioids can influence the *hypothalamus* to reduce the amounts of *cortisol* and *testosterone* in the blood. Pupils contract with opioid use and the veins in the skin widen, giving the upper part of the body a flushed appearance.

Though doctors and scientists today study how opioids work and how they affect the body, people didn't always know or care about the scientific facts behind the drugs. All they cared about was the fact that the drugs ended their pain and allowed them to escape from the world for a little while. Opioids have been around for thousands of years, and it is only recently that we have started wondering how and why these drugs work instead of simply accepting their effects.

The National Institute on Drug Abuse lists some of the uses and consequences of opioids in its 2005 report:

Use and Consequences of Opioids

Opioids
- oxycodone
- propoxyphene
- hydrocodone
- hydromorphone
- meperidine
- diphenoxylate
- morphine
- codeine
- fentanyl
- methadone

Generally prescribed for
- postsurgical pain relief
- management of acute or chronic pain
- relief of cough and diarrhea

Effects of short-term use
- alleviates pain
- drowsiness
- constipation
- depressed respiration (depending on dose)

Effect of long-term use
- potential for physical dependence and addiction

Possible negative effects
- severe respiratory depression or death following a large single dose

Should not be used with other substances that cause central nervous system depression, including:
- alcohol
- antihistamines
- barbiturates
- benzodiazepines
- general anesthetics

(*Source:* From *National Institute on Drug Abuse Research Report,* August 2005)

Prescription Drug Statistics

- In 2009, almost 5.3 million persons aged 12 or older had used prescription pain relievers nonmedically at least once in the month before the survey.
- Nonmedical use of prescription pain relievers accounted for 17.1 percent of first-time illicit drug use among persons twelve or older.
- The numbers of persons using prescription pain relievers nonmedically for the first time increased from 600,000 in 1990 to 2.2 million in 2009.
- About 1.9 million persons aged 12 or older were dependent on or abused prescription pain relievers in 2009.

(*Source: The NSDUH Report,* 2009.)

Canadian Opioid Abuse

According to Canadian statistics, the nonmedical use of opioid painkillers in Canada has increased at such a staggering rate since the late 1990s, that these users outnumber street heroin users in some treatment populations. Because of the rampant abuse of these drugs, officials are finding it difficult to curtail their illegal use while making certain that they remain available for those who truly need them.

Current estimates suggest that there are almost 85,000 regular opioid users in Canada.

(Source: "An overview of illegal opioid use and health services utilization in Canada," S. Popova.)

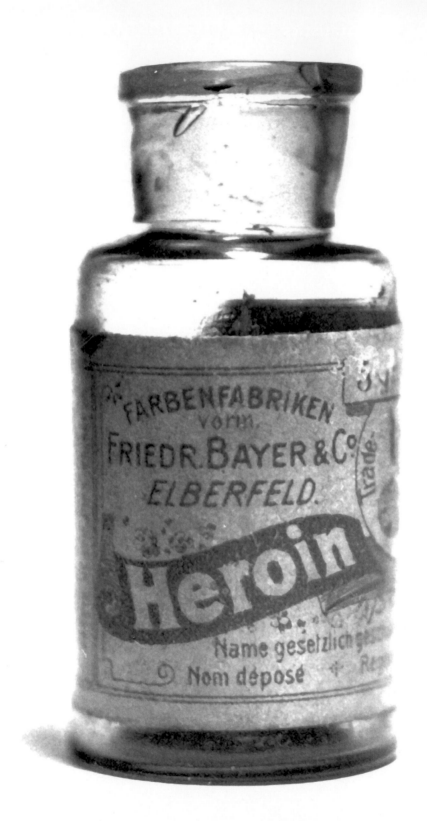

2 The History of Opioids

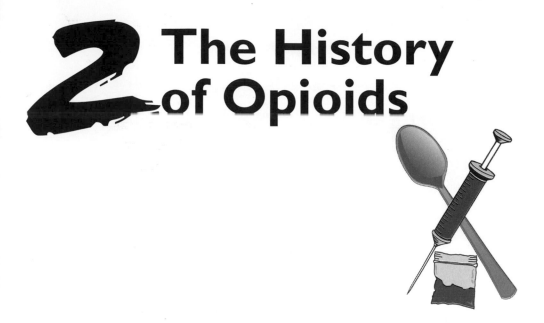

In 1839, Lin Tse-hsu, of China, wrote the following letter to Queen Victoria, the ruler of Great Britain:

> After a long period of commercial intercourse, there appear among the crowd of barbarians both good persons and bad, unevenly. Consequently there are those who smuggle opium to seduce the Chinese people and so cause the spread of the poison to all provinces. Such persons who only care to profit themselves, and disregard their harm to others, are not tolerated by the laws of heaven and are unanimously hated by human beings. His Majesty the Emperor, upon hearing of this, is in a towering rage. He has especially sent me, his commissioner, to come to Kwangtung, and together with the governor-general and governor jointly to investigate and settle this matter.

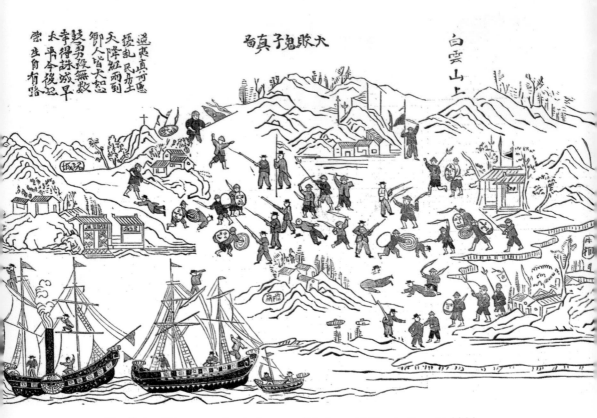

The Opium Wars were fought between Britain and China in the mid-1800s. They were the result of a disagreement over the importation of opium into China.

All those people in China who sell opium or smoke opium should receive the death penalty. If we trace the crime of those barbarians who through the years have been selling opium, then the deep harm they have wrought and the great profit they have usurped should fundamentally justify their execution according to law. We take into consideration, however, the fact that the various barbarians have still known how to repent their crimes and return to their allegiance to us by taking the

20,183 chests of opium from their store ships and petitioning us, through their consular officer [superintendent of trade], Elliot, to receive it. It has been entirely destroyed and this has been faithfully reported to the Throne in several memorials by this commissioner and his colleagues.

Fortunately we have received a specially extended favor from His Majesty the Emperor, who considers that for those who voluntarily surrender there are still some circumstances to palliate their crime, and so for the time being he has magnanimously excused them from punishment. But as for those who again violate the opium prohibition, it is difficult for the law to pardon them repeatedly. Having established new regulations, we presume that the ruler of your honorable country, who takes delight in our culture and whose disposition is inclined towards us, must be able to instruct the various barbarians to observe the law with care. It is only necessary to explain to them the advantages and disadvantages and then they will know that the legal code of the Celestial Court must be absolutely obeyed with awe.

We find that your country is sixty or seventy thousand li [three li make one mile] from China. Yet there are barbarian ships that strive to come here for trade for the purpose of making a great profit. The wealth of China is used to profit the barbarians. That is to say, the great profit made by barbarians is all taken from the rightful share of China. By what right do they then in return use the poisonous drug to injure the Chinese people? Even though the barbarians may not necessarily intend to do us harm, yet in coveting profit to an extreme, they have no regard for injuring others. Let us ask, where is your conscience? I have heard that the smoking of opium is very strictly forbidden by your country; that is because the harm caused by opium is clearly understood. Since it is not permitted to do harm to your own country, then even less should you let it be passed on to the harm of other countries—how much less to China!

Clearly, more than a hundred and fifty years ago, opioids were already creating problems for both individuals and societies. The Opium Wars between China and England brought this problem to the forefront of history—but opium was not a newcomer on the world stage.

The seed of the poppy has been used since prehistoric times; evidence of the plants have been found in Neolithic settlements in Switzerland in the form of poppy-seed cakes and the seedpods of the plant that date back

Poppy seeds and their oil have been used in cooking for thousands of years. Archaeologists have found seed cakes and seedpods in Neolithic settlements.

Heroin and Other Opioids—Poppies' Perilous Children 31

In Homer's Odyssey, Telemachus is given a drink of wine mixed with opium. According to Homer, this was to rid Telemachus of the pain and grief for his missing father, Odysseus.

more than 4,000 years. While archaeologists conjecture that the plant was used for nutritional value—the seeds contain oil that can be used for cooking purposes—it is also probable and even likely that these early cultures had discovered the plant's narcotic effects.

Early History

The first opioid that was discovered and used was opium, as it is the crudest form of the drug and the easiest to make. The word "opium" derives from a Greek word meaning "juice of a plant" and refers to the fact that opium is made by drying the sap found in the seedpod of the poppy. As the origin of the word implies, the first mention of opium was in Greece. In the third century BCE, the philosopher Theophrastus referred to the drug in his writings. Homer also talks about the effects of opium in his epic *The Odyssey*.

Greece was not the only country that used the poppy plant. Civilizations in Mesopotamia, Persia, and Egypt also cultivated the bright red flower. There, the plant was known as *hul gil*, or plant of joy. In Egypt, priests—who also served as doctors—encouraged families to grow their own poppies. Egyptian pharaohs were entombed with poppies or opium to take with them to the next world. Arabic doctors, who discovered opium from Rome, used opium to relieve pain. In fact, it became a popular drug in Arabia, where Muslims were forbidden from drinking by Mohammed, but not from using opium. For many Arab Muslims, the drug became a way of escaping from daily life and problems, a recreational drug much like alcohol is for many people today. Traders from Arabic countries spread the drug throughout the Far East and reintroduced it in Europe. By the eighth century CE, opium had spread to India and China as well.

Around the known ancient world, poppies and opium became an integral part of many cultures. **Pictograms** of the poppy are found frequently in Egyptian art and writing. The Greek and Roman gods of sleep, referred to as Hypnos and Somnos, respectively, are often shown in artwork as either wearing or carrying poppies.

Opium in Asia

Today, many people associate opium with the Chinese opium dens of the 1800s. These places abounded in large cities all over the world, and were focal points for both the arts and for crime.

Opium was considered an integral part of Chinese culture. The Chinese had known for centuries of the drug and its effects, and by the nineteenth century, it was considered merely a fact of life. In earlier times, many people either ate parts of the poppy flower, or brewed the flower into a tea or other drink. By the seventh century, the Chinese discovered that the effects of the drug were much more powerful if the juice of the flower was dried and smoked. This was the beginning of opioid use in western Asia.

The habit didn't spread in China, however, until the seventeenth century, when the Dutch brought pipes to the country, allowing people the opportunity to smoke opium with pipes for the first time. Opium pipes varied in size and decoration, ranging from simple bamboo affairs to bejeweled, carved, expensive pieces of fine workmanship. Oftentimes, the opium in the pipes was mixed with Indian tobacco, also brought over by the Dutch.

Even the poor smoked opium in China. Old opium pipes often contained a mixture of charcoal and opium that was referred to as "dross." This could be mixed with more tobacco or other substances and then be sold at a reduced price to those who could not afford real opium.

The Development of Laudanum

As time went on and the use of opium spread to Europe and the United States, people became more and more excited about the miraculous drug that could cure myriad problems. Opium was known by many names, each more flattering than the one before it; the drug was called by

The effects of opium were stronger when the poppy resin was dried and smoked. People gathered to smoke opium from long pipes in places called opium dens.

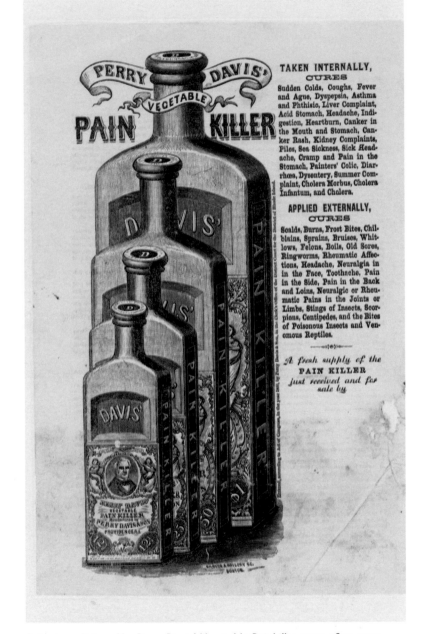

Patent medicines, like Perry Davis' Vegetable Painkiller, were often seen as wonder drugs. However, the ingredients in the "all-natural" elixir were mainly opium and alcohol.

If you had a cough in the eighteenth century, your doctor might have suggested you dose yourself with the following medication: *a teacupful of opium syrup three or four times a day.* Or, if you suffered from headaches, he would have been likely to prescribe an opium powder for you to take. These medicines were all perfectly legal in the 1700s.

Opium was marketed under a variety of labels such as these:

• Ayer's Cherry Pectoral,
• Mrs. Winslow's Soothing Syrup,
• McMunn's Elixer,
• Godfrey's Cordial,
• Hamlin's Wizard Oil,
• Scott's Emulsion, and
• Dover's Powder.

These remedies were advertised as "painkillers," "cough mixtures," "soothing syrups," and "women's friends." They were used to treat everyone from rheumatic grandparents to teething babies. The medicine may have soothed the patients' pain, but as a result many people, including babies, suffered addiction, withdrawal pains, and even death. And yet the medicine was thought to cure diarrhea, colds, cholera, fever, cancer—and even baldness and athlete's foot!

such titles as "the Sacred Anchor of Life," "the Hand of God," and "the Destroyer of Grief."

During the 1700s, opium smoking became quite popular in the Far East. As a result, the cultivation of poppies became a very lucrative business. The English, Dutch, and Spanish all had separate sources of opium. Eventually, the drug became so readily available that it was easy to find and purchase all over the world. People did not yet know that opium use could lead to addiction and other health problems.

Robert Burton, an eighteenth-century scholar and priest, as well as the author of *Anatomy of Melancholy*, recommended laudanum (opium dissolved in wine) for insomnia. Laudanum had first been discovered in the sixteenth century, when Philippus Aureolus Theophrastus Bombastus von Hohenheim (also known as Paracelsus) found that opium dissolves much better in alcohol than in water. The name, laudanum, means "something to be praised," and the original version contained such ingredients as crushed pearls and *frogspawn*, as well as opium. Thomas Sydenham, a physician in the 1680s, was the first to create a standard and consistent recipe for laudanum. Sydenham added opium, saffron, cinnamon, and cloves, and dissolved it all in *canary wine*, thereby making the standard laudanum that was used for centuries.

While laudanum was habit forming, this, as well as some of its other side effects, may have been due in part to the alcohol content of the solution rather than to the opium itself. Tolerance to the opium, however, was what led people to consume greater and greater amounts of the laudanum in search of a high.

By the 1800s, opium and laudanum were available almost anywhere, including pharmacies and grocery stores. It came in various forms now, including laudanum drops and opium *tinctures*. Because of this and the popular culture that stated opioids were real medical cures, its use continued to rise, leading to an even greater increase in opium imports.

Morphine Is Discovered

Opium contains a number of different chemicals, but this was not discovered until 1806, when Friedrich Sertürner

In the 16th century Paracelsus discovered that opium dissolves better in alcohol than water. Laudanum, or opium dissolved in wine, was recommended as a cure for insomnia.

Heroin and Other Opioids—Poppies' Perilous Children 39

Morphine was first isolated in 1804 by Friedrich Sertürner. By the Civil War, the abuse of morphine became so common in the military that the addiction was known as "soldier's disease."

was the first to extract one of these in its pure form. He called his new drug morphine. Codeine was the next to be extracted in 1832, by the pharmacist Pierre-Jean Robiquet. These new opioids replaced raw opium as painkillers in the medical field. The invention of the hypodermic needle spurred popularity in the new discovery, especially in the use of morphine.

Morphine's use skyrocketed during the Civil War when it was used to treat wounds. According to some historians, so many military personnel became addicted to it that morphine dependence was called the "soldier's disease." Doctors and patients both came to rely on the instant relief supplied by morphine. In fact, it was used so often that the 1897 edition of the Sears Roebuck catalog offered a hypodermic kit—a syringe, two needles, two vials, and a handy carrying case for one's personal supply of morphine. The entire kit cost $1.50.

The Use of Opioids in Everyday Life

By the year 1860, opium imports had risen to 280,000 pounds in Britain. Everyone used opium in some way, but the use was concentrated mostly in the rural areas around the Fens and in other country villages. Not only did people use imported opium, most of which came from Turkey, but many people grew their own poppies as well, which they brewed into a tea and used to cure various ailments.

Even young children were given opioids. Opium and other poppy-based drugs were like the **Ritalin** of today; they were used to calm children and keep them quiet and docile. "Medicines" like Godfrey's Cordial, which was used to cure colic, Atkinson's Infants' Preservative, and

Mrs. Winslow's Soothing Syrup all became popular during this time, and they all contained opioids.

Nobody seemed to realize that the use of opioids could possibly be harmful or addictive. It was only later, in the late 1800s, that people started trying to curb the use of opioids.

The Opium Wars

Opium played an important role in world history. By 1839, the Chinese government had banned the use and importation of opium. However, a large **black market** still existed for the drug, and it continued to be smuggled into the country. Finally, Emperor Tao Kwang ordered his personal emissary Lin Tse-hsü to stop this problem. Lin Tse-hsü asked Queen Victoria, the Queen of England, for help, but he was ignored. In his fury, Emperor Tao Kwang took over 20,000 barrels of opium and arrested the foreign traders who had been carrying the drug.

Britain reacted by attacking Canton, a port city in China, and the first Opium War started. The Chinese were eventually defeated by the British, who at that time had a tremendous empire from which to draw soldiers and other resources. In 1842, the Chinese signed the Treaty of Nanjing. This document stated that the opium trade would continue in China, that China would pay **reparations** to Britain, that China would **cede** Hong Kong to Britain, and that China would open up five more port cities to international trade. This treaty forced China to abandon its policy of **isolationism** and to deal with other cultures. This was a huge concession for a country that saw itself as, literally, the center of the world at the time.

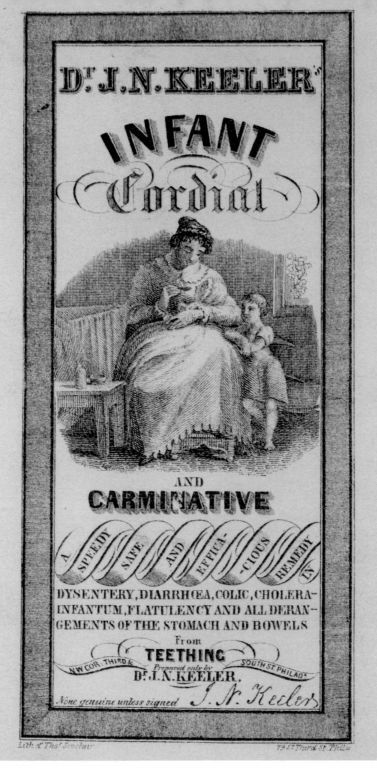

Opioids were used by everyone in the mid to late 1800s. Even infants were given opioids, in the form of soothing syrups and cordials, meant to keep them calm and quiet.

After the second Opium War, Britain and China signed a treaty that allowed the importation of opium into China. By the 1890s almost a quarter of the men in China were addicted.

Not surprisingly, the Chinese were unable to live with the terms of the treaty and peace didn't last. The Second Opium War began in 1856 and lasted less than a year. Again, the war was fought over British demands that China expand its opium markets. Again, Britain's superior military defeated the Chinese. In 1858, another treaty, the Treaty of Tientsin, was signed. This legalized the importation of opium to China. British traders claimed that this treaty was to keep the opium trade regulated and to protect it from being taken over by pirates.

Opium began pouring into the country, and by the 1890s, almost a quarter of the men in China were addicted to the drug.

Opium in the United States

Meanwhile, in North America, no outside power forced the citizens to accept opium as happened in China. Instead, it was a more gradual process. Early settlers brought poppy seeds with them when they crossed the Atlantic Ocean from Europe. Once grown, the raw opium could be dissolved in whisky to provide relief from coughs and other pains.

However, pain relief was not the only way poppy seeds proved useful. The seeds were also used to make birdseed, and poppy seeds are often found on top of rolls and breads, even today. They can also be used as flavoring, and the oil can be used for cooking, as a *condiment*, and even in making soap. Because of the many uses of the plant, Americans all over the country grew the poppy.

Throughout most of the nineteenth century, opium use was high throughout America. Opioids were cheap and readily available. Doctors wrote prescriptions for opioids; many opioids were available over the counter, even in grocery stores and general stores; opioids could be ordered by mail; and many medicines contained opioids, even medicines meant for young children, which were used as remedies for everything from teething to dysentery to "women's trouble."

It wasn't until the late 1800s that Americans started worrying about the ill effects opioids could have on people. Part of this was because of racial *stereotypes*; after all, opium was an important part of the "alien" Chinese culture. When Chinese immigrants moved to the United

States, they were hated, not only because they looked different, but also because they were perceived to be stealing American's jobs. Since opium was a part of these newcomers' lives, American popular opinion swung against the poppy-derived substance. Surely something so dangerously foreign should not be part of American culture! (Despite how Americans felt about Chinese immigrants, it wouldn't be until 1942 that the cultivation of opium poppies was banned in the United States.)

In the late nineteenth century, doctors and scientists had begun to realize the addictive powers of both opium and morphine. As a result, they started searching for a drug with similar effects but with less of a tendency for addiction. In 1874, the English pharmacist C. R. Alder Wright believed that he had come up with a solution; he boiled morphine and acetic acid (the main ingredient in vinegar) together. This new compound, with the chemical name diacetylmorphine, was marketed by Bayer in 1898 and given the commercial name of Heroin. The same manufacturer that would later bring the world aspirin also brought the world heroin.

The Opium Conventions

By 1909, the United States was trying to stop the use and distribution of opium for purposes other than pain relief, both domestically and abroad. As part of this new ideal, American leaders persuaded all the countries with territories in the Far East and Persia to meet. This conference, which took place in Shanghai, was known as the International Opium Conference. It was here that many countries agreed to establish international laws that would govern the preparation and trade of both cocaine and morphine. All countries at the conference were in agreement on

Heroin was created by boiling morphine and acetic acid together. The creator of heroin was searching for a drug with similar effects as opium and morphine but without the addictive qualities.

Heroin and Other Opioids—Poppies' Perilous Children 47

The United Sates was the first country to declare possession of opioids to be illegal. The law has since been expanded to include many other dangerous substances.

48 Chapter 2—The History of Opioids

this point, except for Germany, who worried about losing money due to the huge investments their pharmaceutical companies had made in these drugs.

After many conventions and treaties, the convening nations eventually agreed that all countries should try to control the trade of narcotics within their own, domestic governments. The United States was one of the only countries that implemented this plan, when the government passed the Harrison Narcotics Act of 1914. This law controlled the trade of opioids and pushed forward the idea that it was illegal to have possession of any of these drugs, a concept that has broadened to include many other drugs and illicit substances over the years.

In 1961, the United Nations developed an international treaty called the Single Convention to regulate the use, manufacture, and distribution of opioids, as well as cocaine and cannabis. This was supplemented in 1971 by the international treaty known as the Convention of Psychotropic Substances. The United States passed its own laws under the framework of the Controlled Substances Act in 1971, which provide a means of regulating the use, manufacture, and distribution of opioids and other addictive drugs in a manner consistent with the international treaties. Despite these efforts, the lure of these powerfully addictive drugs, as well as the profits that could be made by their illicit sellers, kept opioid addiction's many forms a continuing challenge to health service providers and crime control.

While the technology behind the processing and development of opioids has grown tremendously, some things are still exactly the same: all kinds of people use opioids, whether for legitimate pain relief or simply in order to achieve a high.

3 Who Uses Opioids?

Rosemarie had known since she was fourteen that she would be a drug addict; by then, she was using opioids at least once a month, normally more, and there was a history of drug and alcohol addiction in her family. Her mother had cancer, and one day, when Rosemarie had a bad headache and there was no ibuprofen left, her mother gave Rosemarie a couple of her pills. Rosemarie loved the feeling. Before long, she found that the pills helped remove her emotional pain as well, at least for a while. Rosemarie was soon using codeine, dihydrocodeine, morphine (the twelve-hour release sort), dextropropoxyphene, hydrocodone, and anything else she could get her hands on.

When Rosemarie's mother died, Rosemarie's drug use increased to once or twice a week. Soon all her mother's pills were gone, but in England (where Rosemarie lived) some opioids were sold over the counter (codeine, dihydrocodeine, and morphine in very small quantities of

As a person becomes more dependent on opioids, other aspects of her life will suffer. For example, a student will probably show a drop in her grades.

approximately 90 milligrams in 300-milliliter bottles of medicine). Rosemarie also managed to get her doctor to prescribe dextropropoxyphene for her—and she stole hydrocodone from her grandmother.

Rosemarie thought her drug use was a piece of cake. Oh, maybe she needed to take more pills to get the same high after a while than she had at first—but she tried to handle that by stopping her drug use for one month every year. Sometimes, she worried that the pharmacist was getting suspicious of all the drugs she was taking. But the drugs were cheap, and everyone knew she was a sickly sort of girl who needed a lot of medicine. And no one really suspected a teenage girl (especially one who looked young for her age) of being an opioid addict.

At school, her grades fell from A's to B's, but everyone just assumed this was due to her mother's death. Her friends suspected something was wrong, but they assumed it was just depression. No one noticed that Rosemarie only wore long sleeves. (She had taken to extracting the morphine from anti-diarrhea medicine and injecting it.)

When Rosemarie was eighteen, she moved to a bigger city, hoping her problems (boredom, depression, and ever-increasing drug use) would magically go away there. For a while at least, they seemed to. She had a new group of friends, she enrolled in college, and she managed to keep her grades up. Best of all, she hardly ever used opioids.

After her final exams, she and her friends decided to celebrate. A group of them wanted to enhance their fun with drugs, so they brought Rosemarie with them to a local dealer. The dealer graciously offered them some heroin (the pharmaceutical sort in *ampules*). At first Rosemarie said no, but her friends kept calling her a chicken, so finally she gave in. When she and her five friends injected the heroin, they noticed how easily Rosemarie found a vein, and they realized she'd had previous experience with injecting. Rosemarie told them about her experiences with opioids; in the end, she was the one who administered all the injections. Rosemarie went along with her friends, but she hated giving the injections; she was pretty sure that at least one of her group would end up an addict.

Over the next few weeks, the group of friends used heroin every weekend. Rosemarie knew better than to slip into the "just this once, I'll be fine" mid-week use, but her five friends didn't. Gradually, they stopped going out with Rosemarie on the weekend. The only time Rosemarie ever saw them now was when they used heroin together.

Although Rosemarie was trying to keep her life together, her professors, employer, and other friends began to treat her with suspicion. Her employer asked her to take drug tests; Rosemarie failed these several times, but each time she convinced him that her positive drug test came from the prescription medicine Paracodol (paracetamol with 8 milligrams of codeine). Rosemarie told him she had to take these tablets for headaches because she was allergic to aspirin and ibuprofen.

Over the next nine months, Rosemarie continued to use heroin, despite the way it complicated the rest of her life. She also found that her skin bruised easily from the frequent injections. However, that didn't stop her. She still used. Rosemarie was addicted.

Rosemarie's story is a true one adapted from www.erowid. org/experiences/exp.php?ID=16385. Like Rosemarie, many people are first introduced to opioids as legitimate medications for pain relief.

A heroin addict who injects regularly will begin to show signs on his arms. He may start wearing only long sleeve shirts to cover the bruises and evidence of injections.

Heroin and Other Opioids—Poppies' Perilous Children   55

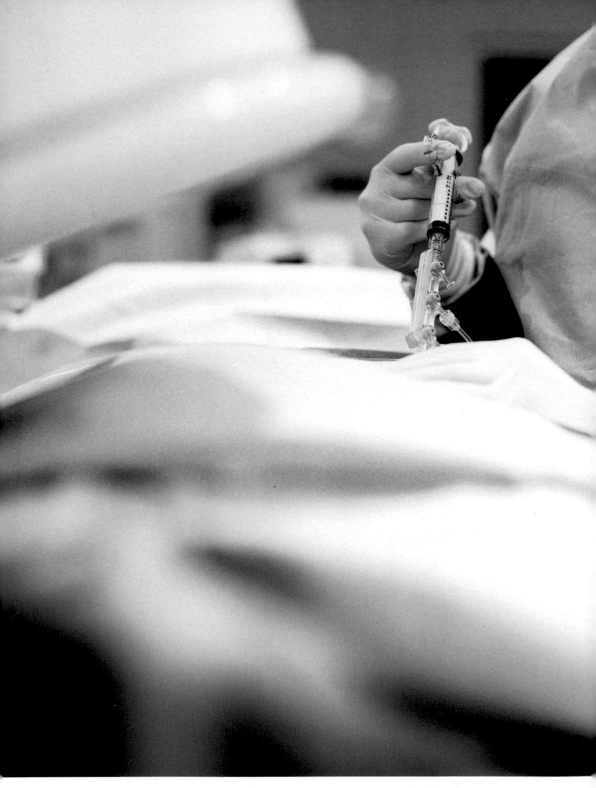

No other medications are as effective at relieving pain as opioids. Therefore, they are used in severe cases, such as during cancer treatment.

Opioids and Pain Relief

Many people use opioids to relieve strong or chronic pain of some sort. No other drugs have been found that are more effective for severe pain, despite research that has attempted to find safer, less addictive drugs for this purpose. This is why almost everyone has used some sort of opioid at one point or another, whether it is morphine after a major surgery, or codeine and Tylenol after getting wisdom teeth removed.

Because of their almost unlimited ability to decrease a patient's pain, opioids are used in such extreme cases as cancer treatment; even disabling pain can be dealt with by using high enough doses of opioids. However, the doses that are necessary to alleviate this pain often lead to tolerance, meaning that a patient has to take even more to achieve the desired effect.

In the United States, opioids are used for several purposes besides pain relief. Various opioids are used for anesthesia during operations. Codeine and hydrocodone are put into cough medicine. Opium can stop diarrhea. Millions of people get relief from their illnesses with some kind of opioid, making them a very useful group of drugs. Unfortunately, these drugs are also used for recreational purposes, which often leads to abuse and addiction.

Recreational Use of Opioids

While all opioids and opioids are abused, the only one without a legitimate medical purpose is heroin. Heroin users, as well as everyone who abuses opioids, are looking for the euphoria that comes when the drugs are consumed at high levels. As tolerance builds, these users continue to use higher and higher levels of the drug in order to feel the original high, the feeling to which they have become addicted.

In 2008, the National Survey on Drug Use and Health (NSDUH) found that 213,000 persons aged twelve or

Percentage of Students Who Think Heroin is Dangerous

% seeing "great risk" in using once or twice

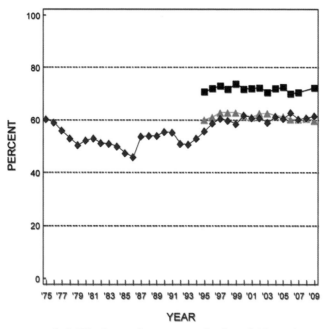

On average, only 0.8% of teens between grades 9 and 12 use heroin; most consider it too dangerous to try even once.

older in the United States had used heroin in the month prior to the survey. This number represented an increase of 60,000 over the survey's findings in 2008. The 2009 survey reported that, in the years 2002 to 2008, anywhere from 91,000 to 118,000 people started taking heroin each year. The average age at first use was 25.5 years in 2009.

While these numbers represent only those people who used heroin once, the 2008 survey also found that 282,000 persons age twelve or older were classified as dependent on heroin. Overdoses are a problem as well; in 2009 there were more than 213,000 emergency room visits due to the overdose or use of heroin.

Opioids and Teens

In 2010, a Monitoring the Future study was done that tried to measure the drug use of teens around the United States. This survey, found that 1.3 percent of students in grades eight, and ten had tried heroin in their lifetime. The same study found that 1.6 percent of students in grade twelve had tried heroin in their lifetime. However, a different study, this one done by the Centers for Disease Control and Prevention (CDC) in the United States, found the percentage of students who had tried heroin to be higher; over 3 percent of teens between the grades of nine and twelve. Luckily, this statistic has decreased since the year 2001, going from 3.1 percent to 2.4 percent. The majority of students think that the risks of heroin outweigh the benefits; 61.4 percent of eighth-graders, 72.4 percent of tenth-graders, and 60.5 percent of twelfth-graders thought that using heroin, even once or twice, without a needle was a "great risk."

Heroin is an expensive addiction. Many dependent users turn to criminal acts in an attempt to get the money they need to buy more heroin.

60 Chapter 3—Who Uses Opioids?

Opioids and Crime

Opioids are often involved in crimes as well. Whether criminals are arrested as they attempt to rob or steal to pay for their habit, or whether the drug is only the root cause of a perpetrator's behavior, around 6 percent of arrestees test positive for opioids. This finding is based on a study done by the Arrestee Drug Abuse Monitoring (ADAM) Program, which discovered that around 5.8 percent of males and 6.6 percent of females tested positive for heroin at the time of arrest. Another 5 percent of males said that they had used heroin within a year of their arrest.

These same criminals, taken from many different test sites all around the United States, were often frequent users. It is very unlikely that someone will be arrested while high if they are simply experimenting. Of the men and women who described themselves as frequent users, all of them had taken heroin an average of ten of the previous thirty days. That means that these people were using heroin every three days and had a heavy habit to support.

Not all heroin users who commit crimes set out to hurt people. Many are simply trying to get funds to satisfy their drug habits; heroin is expensive, especially when it is used more than once a week. However, heroin can lead a person deeper and deeper into a life of crime—and eventually, in many cases, the person ends up serving years in prison.

The legal consequences are not the only issue opioid users face; there are many physical side effects as well. While some are merely annoying or troublesome, others can be life threatening.

4 The Dangers of Opioids

After Derek had spent his adolescence staying away from drugs and being generally "good," he decided that now that he was in his twenties, he wanted to try every drug there was. He started off with marijuana, and worked his way up from there. He wanted to be able to say that he'd done them all.

One cold, rainy night, he and his friends Steve and Greg were sitting in Derek's apartment, trying to think of something to do. It was too cold and wet to go out, and finally, Derek decided he would walk down the street to buy some weed from a dealer he knew. Derek bought twenty bucks' worth of weed off the guy; then, on the spur of the moment, Derek asked him if he had any heroin. The dealer did; it was only ten bucks a hit, he told Derek.

Derek ran back through the rain to his apartment and told his friends how cheap the heroin was. "We should try it! It will be one more drug to add to our list." They were all doing their best to have the longest list—plus they wanted to "expand their consciousness" in as many ways as possible.

Derek bought two hits, opened up one, and poured out the contents onto a CD gem box. He used a Metrocard to chop up the small, light brown chunks, then he divided the small amount of powder into two lines about an inch and a half long. He sat there for a moment, almost over-come with awe at what he was about to do. Heroin: that was the real thing in his book, the ultimate high. But he couldn't help feeling a little scared.

Eventually, Derek got up his nerve to take a straw he had cut into thirds and snort a line. It burned the inside of his nostril a little, and it smelled like dust. Derek knew that smell probably meant the heroin had been cut with some other substance, but he didn't want to think about what it could be.

He only snorted one line, and then he waited for about fifteen minutes. Not much happened, though, just a feeling of warmth that slowly crept over him. He sat on the couch next to Greg, feeling relaxed and happy, until he realized he could probably feel something even better than this warm fuzzy feeling—so he snorted the rest of the powder and waited. Twenty minutes later, Derek was out of it.

Derek felt so good, so comfortable, that he already knew he wanted to repeat the experience. During that first euphoric hour, he thought about how nice it would be to do this once a week, or on special occasions. Then the itching started.

Derek's entire body felt like an enormous mosquito bite. He rolled on the floor, scratching himself and

Heroin can be found in a number of different forms. The powder form varies from brown to white, and often has other substances added.

Heroin and Other Opioids—Poppies' Perilous Children 65

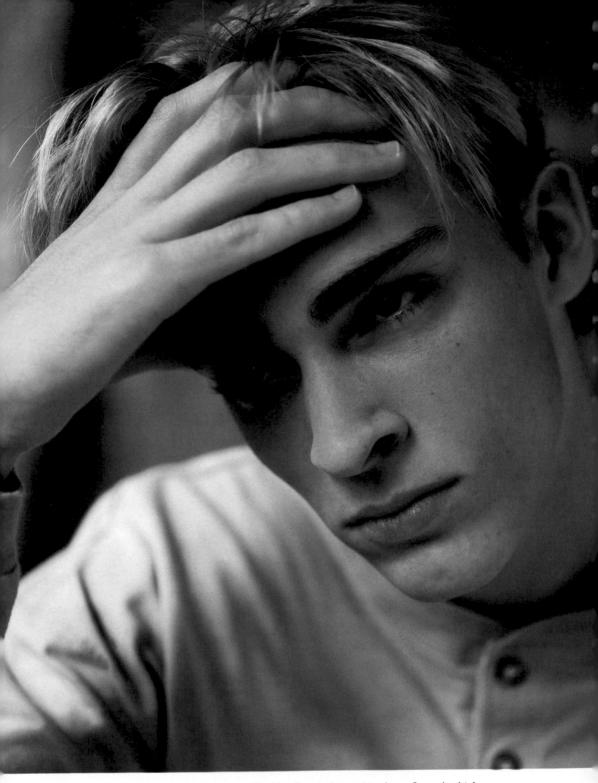

One of the negative aspects of taking heroin is coming down from the high. Though everyone is affected differently, severe headaches that may last for days are common.

66 Chapter 4—The Dangers of Opioids

screaming at Greg and Steve. Suddenly, he hated Greg; his voice was like nails on a blackboard. His friend Steve was getting on his nerves too, the way he just sat there, and Derek realized he hated Steve. Then his itching stopped, and he felt better than ever.

Greg and Derek lay on the bed and talked about weird things, while Steve passed out on the couch. Greg and Derek eventually stopped talking and went into a strange, dreamy state, filled with bizarre and vivid thoughts. It was a pleasant feeling, like floating in a dream. Everything was warm, and Derek's bed, blanket, and pillows seemed like the most comfortable, wonderful creations ever made. Derek didn't want it to end.

After the three friends had lain around in coma-like states for three hours, Derek started to come down. It wasn't unpleasant, except that he was suddenly freezing. Shivering so hard he could hardly walk, he crawled back into bed and fell asleep. He woke up every twenty minutes or so, drenched in sweat, completely soaked. This went on all night.

In the morning, Derek's entire body ached. When he went out to run some errands, he could barely walk. He felt like an old man, with a body twisted up with arthritis. He could barely negotiate the subway stairs, and when he got home, he went back to bed and slept the rest of the day. Steve came in and woke him up, but Derek could barely move.

The next day wasn't any better, and he stayed in bed all day. He woke up in the evening, his headache finally gone. However, he was still nauseated and felt feverish and chilled at the same time, as though he had the flu.

For the next week, every time Derek thought about heroin, his stomach would turn. He had never felt so weak and sick before, and it scared him. He doesn't want to try heroin ever again. It just wasn't a fun drug. "No thanks," he says.

Derek's story is true, based on his account on www. erowid.org/experiences/exp.php?ID=11470. The side effects he experienced are not unusual.

Short-Term Side Effects

With heroin and other opioids, as with most other drugs, there are many side effects that make themselves known almost immediately after taking the drug. These can vary in intensity and how long it takes to feel them, depending on how one uses the drug. For example, intravenous injections are the quickest way to get anything into one's bloodstream. This means that a user who injects heroin or morphine will feel the effects much quicker and more strongly than someone who ingests the drug. The difference can be extreme; users who take the drug intravenously can feel the effects within seven seconds while ingesting it orally can take up to ten or fifteen minutes.

The reason most people take opioids is to get the euphoric feeling—the high—that comes along with the drug. However, this is not the only effect opioids have on the body. Besides feeling calm and happy, many users of heroin report having a dry mouth and a heavy feeling in all their extremities. Mental functioning becomes clouded and breathing slows as the drug depresses the central nervous system. Other side effects from opioids may include nausea, vomiting, and restlessness. Hunger and thirst are decreased, as is the sex drive.

There are also other psychological effects besides the initial euphoria. Opioid use has been connected with

The effects of heroin depend on how it enters the bloodstream. A user who injects heroin with a needle will feel the effects faster than one who snorts it.

Heroin and Other Opioids—Poppies' Perilous Children

Some people take heroin, a sedative, with cocaine, a stimulant. Called "speed balling," the practice is more dangerous than taking either drug by itself.

mood swings, **lethargy**, and depression. It can also cause such disorders as **anorexia**. While many users of opioids are more likely to deal with increased social and emotional problems than the average person, this is in part due to the conditions under which many users, especially heroin users, live. The constant threat of disease and violence, as well as poor living conditions, combine to make it hard for anyone to live a stable life.

Some users combine heroin or another opioid with cocaine, a practice called "speed balling." Thus, combined with any side effects from the opioid, one must deal with problems from the cocaine as well. This can also be more dangerous, as drugs taken in combination tend to magnify their side effects. For example, taking alcohol with marijuana, or any other drug, can be much more dangerous than drinking alcohol by itself. In this way, the opioid and the cocaine serve to magnify the effects of each other in what may easily be a deadly combination. The user combines a stimulant with the narcotic to cancel the effects of the drugs; the cocaine keeps a user from falling asleep or succumbing to the lethargy the narcotic brings on, and the opioid helps control the hyperactiveness that often occurs when cocaine is ingested.

Long-Term Effects of Opioids

There are many, more harmful effects that can occur when a person uses opioids for extended periods of time. Chronic users of heroin often have collapsed veins due to the constant injections. Heart infections, both in the lining and in the valves themselves, are also possible. Pneumonia may develop as well. This lung inflammation can be fatal when the immune system is already compromised, as in the case of someone living with HIV/AIDS.

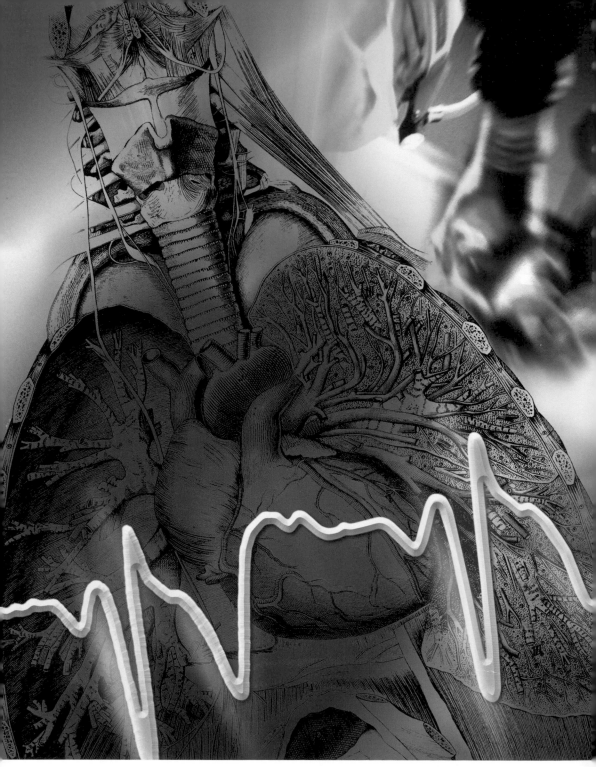

The greatest risk of taking heroin is the possibility of respiratory depression. With repeated uses of heroin, breathing and heart rate can slow so much that they stop.

The most serious side effect, however, for both heroin and other opioids, is the possibility of respiratory depression. While this can occur with a single dose, the tolerance that leads people to take more and more of the drug at a time makes this more likely to occur after repeated use. Respiratory depression, or the slowing down of the breathing rate, can be fatal, as the lungs and heart can slow down until they stop.

Opioids that are not injected lead to side effects of their own, although they are not as dangerous as those that can arise with injection. The immune system is often suppressed, leading to an increased susceptibility to common illnesses like colds or the flu. The endocrine system can become disrupted. Another common problem is constipation. If this condition lasts long enough, it may lead to a bowel obstruction, fecal impaction, or paralytic ileus, which is paralysis of the intestine.

Not only does the drug itself lead to problems, but heroin and other opioids that are sold on the street often contain additives. These may not only be poisonous to the body, but they are often not as soluble as the drug itself is. This can cause foreign chemicals to become clogged in the bloodstream, especially in the blood vessels leading to the lungs, brain, kidneys, heart, or other vital organs. Not only can this cause serious problems like a heart attack, but it can also lead to infection or cell death in these organs.

Other causes of unwanted side effects are the needles used too inject heroin and morphine. These are often less than hygienic and can carry germs that lead to serious diseases. Many heroin users, especially those who live on the streets and with already compromised health systems, cannot afford to buy new needles every time they

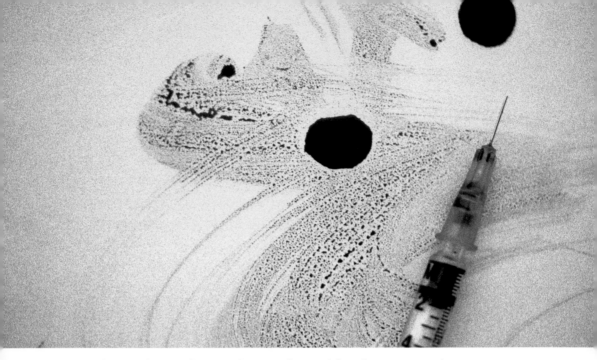

Another danger of injecting heroin is the possibility of contracting a disease from an infected needle. When users share needles, they also share tiny amounts of blood, which can contain thousands of particles of Hepatitis, HIV or tetanus.

shoot up. So, they often share needles, increasing the risk of spreading serious illnesses through the direct reuse of needles or by the exchange of bodily fluids carried on the needles or passed along through sexual intercourse. These illnesses can also be transmitted from a mother to her unborn child.

Liver Diseases, Tetanus, and HIV/AIDS

Hepatitis B is a serious disease caused by a virus that attacks the liver. The virus, which is called hepatitis B virus (HBV), can cause lifelong infection, cirrhosis (scarring) of the liver, liver cancer, liver failure, and death. Hepatitis C is a liver disease caused by the hepatitis C virus (HCV), which is found in the blood of persons who have the disease. HCV is spread by contact with the blood of

Hepatitis A, B, and C: Learn the Differences

	Hepatitis A (HAV)	Hepatitis B (HBV)	Hepatitis C (HCV)
How is it spread?	• found in feces of people with HAV • spread through close personal contact • also spread through contaminated food or water	• found in blood and body fluids • spread through unprotected sex, unclean needles, or during birth • exposure to infected blood in ANY situation is a risk	• found in blood and body fluids • spread through unclean needles, from mother to baby during birth • sometimes spread through unprotected sex
Who is at risk?	• housemates of infected persons • sex partners of infected • children in certain regions of the U.S. • travelers to at risk countries • homosexual men • injecting drug users	• persons with multiple sex partners at once • homosexual men • sex partners of infected persons • injecting drug users • housemates of infected persons • immigrants from at risk areas • healthcare workers who might be exposed to blood	• injecting drug users • recipients of clotting factors made before 1987 • hemodialysis patients • recipients of blood or organ transplants before 1992 • infants born to HCV-infected mothers • though rarely spread through sex, having sex with multiple persons increases risk for HCV
Diagnosis	• have blood tested for HAV, HBV or HCV infection • symptoms of all include jaundice, fever, appetite loss, fatigue, dark urine, joint pain, abdominal pain, diarrhea, nausea, and vomiting		
	• incubation period of 15 to 50 days • one time infection	• incubation period of 45 to 160 days • can be a chronic infection	• incubation period of 14 to 180 days • usually a chronic infection
Treatment	• no treatment • avoid alcohol	• have liver checked every 6-12 months • antiviral medications • liver transplant • avoid alcohol	• have liver checked every 6-12 months • combination therapy 50% effective • vaccination • avoid alcohol
Prevention	• vaccine • after recent exposure get a dose of immune globulin • always wash hands after using the bathroom, changing a diaper and when working with food	• vaccine • infants born to HBV mothers should receive vaccine within 12 hours of birth • always use latex condoms during sexual encounters	• no vaccine • use condoms
		• do not share razors, toothbrushes or washcloths (might have blood on them) • consider the risks of getting a tattoo or body piercing • healthcare workers should follow routine barrier precautions • don't inject drugs; if you do, do not share needles • If you have HBV or HCV do not donate blood or organs	

an infected person. A drop of blood so minuscule that it cannot be detected by the human eye may contain hundreds or even thousands of hepatitis B and/or C particles. Even meticulous cleaning may not totally eradicate from a needle the viruses that cause these serious liver diseases.

Tetanus (sometimes referred to as lockjaw) is a serious but preventable disease that affects the body's muscles and nerves. It is usually spread from a skin wound that becomes contaminated by a bacterium often found in soil. Most cases of tetanus in North America follow a cut or deep puncture injury—such as a wound caused by stepping on a nail—but skin punctures from nonsterile needles (such as with drug use) can also spread the bacteria. Once the bacteria are in the body, they produce a neurotoxin (a protein that acts as a poison to the body's nervous system) that causes muscle spasms. The toxin first affects nerves controlling the muscles near the wound, but it can also travel through the bloodstream and lymph system to other parts of the body. As it circulates through the body, the toxin interferes with the normal activity of nerves, leading to generalized muscle spasms. Without treatment, tetanus can be fatal.

HIV/AIDS is also a possibility that is all too common for heroin users. HIV stands for the human immunodeficiency virus, a retrovirus. Retroviruses integrate and take over a cell's own genetic material. Once taken over, the new cell, now infected with HIV, begins to produce new HIV retroviruses. HIV replicates in the T cells, the body's main defense against illness, and eventually kills them. HIV is only spread through:

- unprotected sexual contact (without using a condom)
- direct inoculation of the virus through contaminated needles

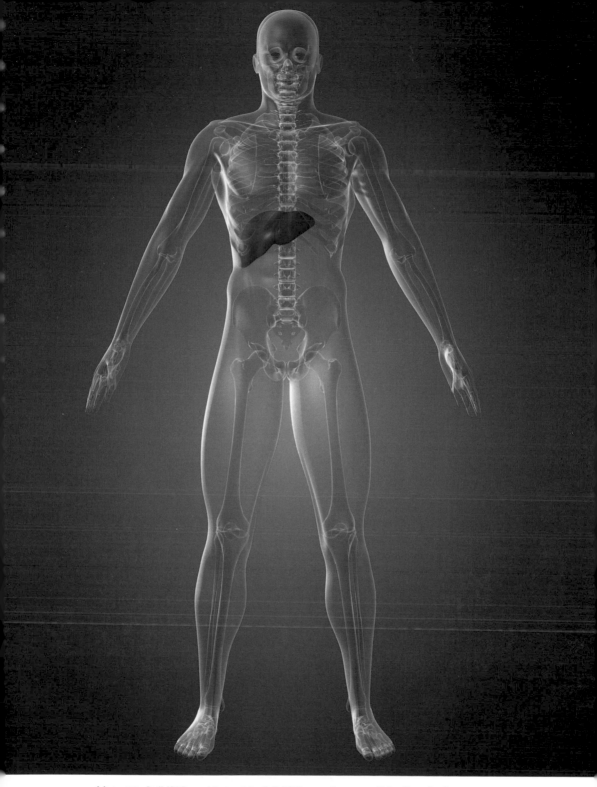

Hepatitis B (HBV) and hepatitis C (HCV) are diseases of the liver. Both can cause serious damage, lifelong infection, and scarring of the liver.

Heroin and Other Opioids—Poppies' Perilous Children 77

XP

OCT-2005

If used properly, latex condoms will help to reduce the risk of transmission of HIV infection (AIDS) and many other sexually transmitted diseases (STD). Also highly effective against pregnancy.

BEFORE USING, READ DIRECTIONS AND WARNINGS ON CARTON OR PRODUCT INSERT.

Imported and Distributed by:
Carter-Horner Inc. Mississauga, ON Canada L5N 1L9
® Registered trademark of Carter-Wallace, Inc.

Lubrifié   Lubricated

Si utilisés selon le mode d'emploi, les condoms de latex contribuent à réduire les risques de transmission du virus VIH (SIDA) et de nombreuses autres maladies transmises sexuellement (MTS). Également très efficaces pour prévenir la grossesse.

HIV can only be spread via the transfer of bodily fluids as through contaminated needles or unprotected sexual contact. Thus, sharing needles or having sex without a condom puts you at risk for HIV.

- contaminated blood products/transplanted organs (In the United States, all donated blood has been tested for HIV since 1985.)
- An infected mother may pass the virus to her developing fetus during the birth or through her breast milk, though treatment of the mother during her pregnancy greatly reduces this means of transmission.

In the first one to three months after a person is infected with the HIV virus is when that person is most *infectious* (that is, the amount of virus in her system is at its highest and T-cell counts are at their lowest). During this time, the body has not had time to react to the virus and produce an adequate immune response to start suppressing HIV. More and more HIV viruses are produced and then released by a process known as budding; when someone becomes infected with the HIV virus, it begins to attack his immune system. This process is not visible, and the individual may not even know she is infected; someone who is infected can look and feel perfectly well for many years. As the disease progresses, the immune system weakens, and the person will become more vulnerable to illnesses the body's defense mechanism would normally have been able to fight. As time goes by, individuals with HIV are likely to become ill more often and develop AIDS.

When HIV infection becomes advanced, it often is referred to as AIDS, acquired immunodeficiency syndrome. AIDS derived its name because:

- It is "acquired"; in other words, it is a condition that has to be *contracted*. It cannot be inherited or transmitted through the genes.
- It affects the body's immune system, the part of the body that fights off diseases.
- It is considered a "deficiency" because it makes the immune system stop working properly.
- It was originally considered a syndrome because people with AIDS experience a number of different symptoms and *opportunistic* diseases.

AIDS is characterized by the appearance of opportunistic infections, which take advantage of a weakened immune system. They include:

- *pneumocystis carinii pneumonia*
- *toxoplasmosis*
- *tuberculosis*
- extreme weight loss and wasting, often made worse by diarrhea
- meningitis and other brain infections
- fungal infections

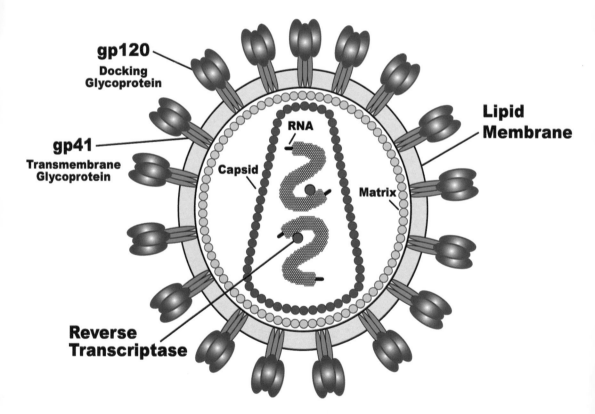

Though most people are familiar with the term AIDS, HIV is actually a more accurate term. HIV refers to the pathogen itself, rather than to a collection of symptoms.

- syphilis
- malignancies such as **lymphoma**, cervical cancer, and **Kaposi's sarcoma**

Although nearly everyone in the world knows the term acquired immunodeficiency syndrome or AIDS, this condition is actually a disease and not a syndrome. A syndrome is commonly used to refer to collections of symptoms that do not have an easily identifiable cause; when the term AIDS was first used, doctors were only aware of the late stages of the disease and did not fully understand its mechanisms. A more current name for the condition, regardless of an AIDS diagnosis, is HIV disease. This name is more accurate because it refers to the **pathogen** that causes AIDS and encompasses all the condition's stages, from infection to the deterioration of the immune system and the onset of opportunistic diseases. However, AIDS is still the name that most people use to refer to the immune deficiency caused by HIV. It is a real and deadly danger for heroin users who exchange needles.

Tolerance to Opioids

Tolerance to any drug refers to the user's inability to achieve the desired high with the same dosage he started out with. Because of this, users will continually raise the doses of a drug that they take in order to feel like they did the first time they used it. This can be dangerous, as the more of the drug that is put in the body, the greater the chances of unwanted side effects or even overdose.

Tolerance also leads to addiction. Finding the drug and getting the high become a user's main goals in life.

A person who is addicted to opioids may have withdrawal symptoms as soon as a few hours after her last dose. Symptoms can include muscle and bone pain, restlessness, vomiting, chills, diarrhea, and cramps.

After a while, the user becomes dependent on the drug, not only mentally but also physically: her body is literally incapable of living without it.

If someone who is addicted to opioids tries to suddenly stop using, withdrawal will occur. This happens when the body tries to make up for the lack of the chemical that it has grown used to, even to the point of needing the drug in order to function. When an addiction is bad enough, withdrawal may occur even a few hours after the drug was last taken. Symptoms include muscle and bone pain, restlessness, vomiting, chills, diarrhea, and twitches in the lower extremities. Depending on the type of opioid, symptoms can also include runny eyes and nose, anxiety, sweating, and cramps. While these symptoms will peak at around twenty-four to forty-eight hours after last ingesting the opioid, they may last for weeks. The speed depends on the **half-life** of the opioid—or how long the drug stays in the body. Although the symptoms of heroin withdrawal are more severe, they are over quickly. Withdrawal from other opioids takes longer but is not as painful. Most of the time the withdrawal symptoms aren't strong enough to kill, except in the case of newborns or unborn fetuses.

Opioids reduce the level of hormones in the body, which in extreme cases can lead to infertility in both men and women. However, it is more likely to lead to birth defects, **spontaneous abortions**, premature births, and **stillbirths**. Opioid addiction also leads to an increase in **SIDS, sudden infant death syndrome**. Babies born to a mother addicted to opioids are born addicted themselves and will go through withdrawal upon being born.

Since these withdrawal symptoms are not generally life threatening to a healthy adult, many users will go through them more than once. Once the drug is flushed out of their system, they can again experience a strong "rush". Some use this as a way to stop the tolerance they are building up to the opioid and to get a better high.

Overdose

Overdose is the worst possible danger of opioids. It is also the most common. Users quickly develop a tolerance to the drug, especially to heroin, that leads them to take higher and higher doses. Eventually, the doses are high enough to kill. In this case, the breathing rate is depressed until breathing stops completely. While some overdoses are due to taking a lethal amount of a drug, others are caused by combining heroin with another drug. The chemical composition of heroin varies from batch to batch, so a user never knows how much heroin she is actually getting in a dose. Therefore, an amount that barely gave someone a high one day may be enough to kill her the next week.

Many overdose deaths occur with previously used doses of opioids because of the presence of other drugs that work in lethal harmony with the opioids to shut down the respiratory system. The most common deadly interaction is with alcohol, but other sedating drugs can also team up with opioids to stop breathing and kill the user.

Since 2006, deaths from heroin overdose have been increasing in the United States. Across the country heroin deaths increased by 20.3 percent from 2006 to 2008. This spike in overdose deaths is blamed on black-tar heroin, an extra-strong type of heroin that is cheap and so pure it can kill users instantly. In 2007, the Centers for Disease Control reported 2,000 deaths related to heroin.

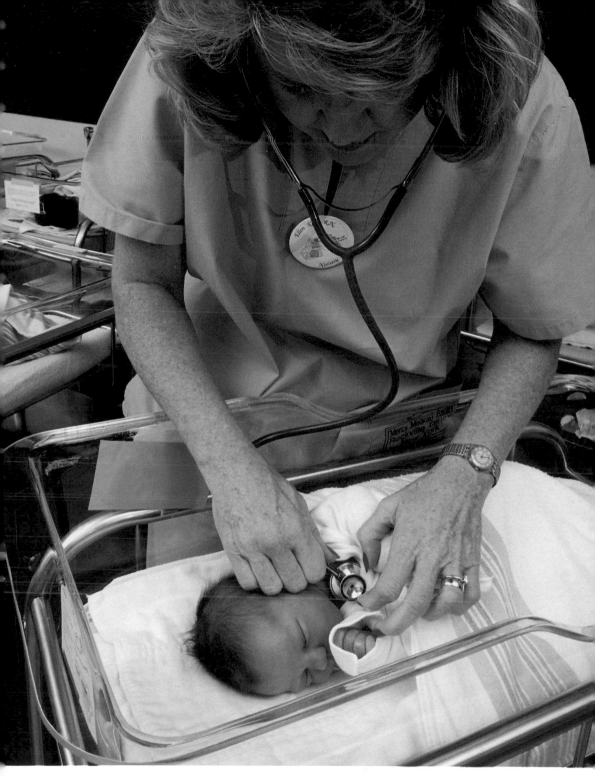

Opioids can lead to infertility in both men and women. If a user does conceive, she runs the risk of seriously harming her baby if she continues getting high while pregnant.

Heroin and Other Opioids—Poppies' Perilous Children 85

As a heroin user gets more addicted to the drug, he needs to take higher and higher doses to feel the same high. Eventually, this can lead to an overdose, which can prove fatal.

Sometimes, however, overdoses occur for no apparent reason. These seem to be caused by an almost-overnight loss of tolerance to the drug. While there are no proven reasons for these odd occurrences, one scientist, Shepard Siegel, developed a hypothesis. Basing his findings on tests he did on rats in a laboratory, he suggested that taking heroin in places that are new or under unusual circumstances has the capability to lessen tolerance to the drug. His findings are backed up not only by the experiments he carried out, but also by the fact that many heroin users overdose in hospitals—an unfamiliar and new place. Also, many addicts who have suffered from a near death due to overdose report that their schedule was different or unusual on the day they overdosed; they did something different or their circumstances were unusual.

Health issues are not the only things that opioid users have to worry about. While many opioids are legal in medical situations, all are illegal when they are abused or used to get high. The most commonly abused opioid, heroin, is not legal in any situation. Therefore, most users not only have to deal with addiction and the problems that may cause, but they may face jail time as well if they are caught in possession of these illegal substances.

5 The Legal Consequences of Using Opioids

Lamar's heroin use started one day when his dealer was out of cocaine. Lamar and his girlfriend were looking to get high—so when he ran into an old buddy who said he could get some heroin, Lamar agreed. He took the white powder home and chopped up two small lines of it for himself and his girlfriend. "The buzz was great," he said later—despite the fact that "it made both of us puke our guts out."

After a couple of weeks went by of snorting dope every day, Lamar realized the new pastime was getting expensive. "Every time my girlfriend would snort a line," he recalled, "she would puke it up and lose her buzz. And, of course, she would want another one. That's when that same old buddy told me that by using a needle, you get a way better high and you wouldn't waste any. I tried it once and I was hooked. My girlfriend refused to inject, so I told her that I wouldn't give her any more dope

Becoming addicted to heroin is dangerous for your health, but it is also very expensive. Many addicts turn to stealing money to get the fix that they need.

because she was wasting it by throwing up every time. So she finally agreed, but I had to shoot it in her arm for her because she was too scared to do it herself."

After a couple of months of shooting heroin, Lamar realized he couldn't stop without feeling deathly sick. He lost his job, and his girlfriend wasn't working either; no money was coming in, and he had a very expensive habit to support. He pawned everything he owned, and then he started pawning his mother's belongings, his girlfriend's belongings, and her parents'. He stole checks from his grandmother; he stole money from his girlfriend's parents' cash cards. He got money any way he could to support his habit—but his resources for money were running out. He was desperate, because he didn't know what he was going to do if he couldn't get hold of enough money to buy more heroin.

By New Year's Eve that year, Lamar was so desperate that he went into the house of his girlfriend's parents and took her father's 22-caliber pistol that was hidden in the basement. With the pistol in his jacket pocket, Lamar drove to the local gas station and robbed the place at gunpoint. He came home with almost four hundred dollars, feeling nothing except relief because he knew he had some cash to buy heroin the next day. Lamar's girlfriend, however, was upset when she found out—but she wasn't too upset to join Lamar while he shot up.

Lamar said, "We were good and high for two days until we ran out of money and dope again. So, thinking of how easy that was, I went and robbed that same store two nights later. This time I came out with less than a hundred bucks, enough to last only through that night and into the morning. So, the next afternoon, I went and robbed a different gas station, coming out with over six hundred dollars. I went straight to my dealer and bought five hundred dollars worth of dope (thirteen or fourteen bags). That night I saw myself on the news for these robberies. I flipped out; I didn't know what to do. At four o'clock in the morning, the police raided my girlfriend's parents' house where I was staying and took me into custody. I knew I was going to be sick in jail. There was nothing I could do but sit and be sick. My bail was $100,000, and I had no way to come up with that kind of money. In May, I was sentenced to forty-eight months in prison. With 'good time,' I only had to do thirty-two months."

By the time Lamar was finally released, his girlfriend had hooked up with someone else and had a child. Lamar went back to his family, who forgave him for everything he did in the past. "About a month after I was out," Lamar said,

> I tried heroin again. I was hooked again instantly. A few months into that, I tried kicking the habit by myself and couldn't do it. So I went and got on to the methadone program. Now to this day, I drink my 110 milligrams every day to stay well. I tried using, but it don't do anything but buzz me for about two minutes and then it's gone, so I figured that it isn't even worth it. So now I'm working again full time and trying to get straight again. I was turned on to crack by that same old buddy, the one who got me into heroin. Some friend, huh? So now I'm trying to choose my friends better. I ask myself why didn't I learn my lesson: wasn't prison enough?

Lamar's story, adapted from www.erowid.org/experiences/exp.php?ID=51667, is just one of many instances where heroin use led to prison time. Stealing money to feed a habit is not the only way an addict can be sent to prison, however. Between October 1, 2004, and January 11, 2005, more than 390 court cases related to heroin were tried in American courts. Of these, 97.4 percent involved dealing or trafficking of the drug.

None of the heroin used in the United States and Canada is produced domestically; it all comes from one of four areas around the world: South America, mostly Colombia; Southeast Asia, where most of the heroin is produced in Burma (Myanmar); Southwest Asia, where it is produced in Afghanistan; and Mexico. The importation of the drug into the United States and Canada

Someone who steals to pay for his heroin addiction is likely to end up sentenced to prison. Even if he does not steal, he may end up in prison for possession of an illegal substance.

Heroin and Other Opioids—Poppies' Perilous Children 93

is illegal; criminals who are caught face heavy fines and prison time.

United States Drug Laws

Throughout the last century, the U.S. government has imposed increasingly stricter laws on the sale and use of illicit drugs. However, the federal government was not always involved in drug use. Before 1890, it was the state's responsibility to monitor and control drug use. One of

Though the possession of heroin or other opioids is illegal today, this was not always the case. In fact, before the late 1800s, there were no laws regulating the possession or use of opioids.

the first laws dealing with opioids was passed in San Francisco in 1875. The law made it illegal to smoke opium anywhere except in designated opium dens. However, it was still legal to sell and import the drug.

It was not until 1890 that Congress passed an act attempting to control the use of morphine and other opioids. Congress levied a tax on both morphine and opium, thinking that if people had to pay taxes on their drugs, they would buy less of them, since the cost would be more expensive. This act was reinforced in 1914 by the Harrison Act, which stated that all parties involved in the importation and distribution of opium and cocaine had to register with the federal government and pay special taxes.

In 1909, the Smoking Opium Exclusion Act was passed. This banned the type of opium that was smoked. However, it did nothing to stop the use of medicines that contained opium. This was a landmark case, however; it represented the first time that the federal government had banned the use of something for a non-medical purpose.

In 1924, heroin became illegal with the passing of the Heroin Act. This law banned the possession and manufacture of heroin, even if it was for medical use. Heroin is still the only opioid that has no legitimate legal use.

The Boggs Act was passed in 1951, imposing minimum prison sentences for those who were found guilty of importing or exporting drugs while breaking the laws established by the Harrison Act. In 1956, the Narcotics Control Act made these penalties even harsher.

The Controlled Substance Act in 1970 implemented the classification system for drugs that we still use today. The law brought together many separate drug laws, all dealing with different types of illicit substances, and put them all into one of five schedules, based on the medicinal value and potential for abuse. Heroin and some other opioids are classified as Schedule I, regarded as the most lethal. These drugs have a high potential for abuse, no medical value, and are considered highly dangerous. Raw opium, opium extracts, codeine, hydrocodone, morphine, and some other opioids are Schedule II drugs. This means that while they have a high potential for abuse, there is an accepted medical value, although restrictions should be placed on the use of the drug. These drugs may also lead to dependence, both physically and psychologically.

A breakthrough in opioid addiction treatment in the United States was the Drug Addiction Treatment Act of 2000. This gave doctors the ability to prescribe approved

The federal government first tried to control the use of morphine and other opioids in 1890. Since then, laws against these and other illicit drugs have become increasingly strict.

SCHEDULE I:

Substance has a high potential for abuse, has no medical use in the United States, and has a lack of accepted safety for use under medical supervision.

SCHEDULE II:

Substance has a high potential for abuse, has a currently accepted medical use in the United States with severe restrictions, and abuse may lead to severe psychological or physical dependence.

SCHEDULE III:

Substance has a potential for abuse (less than Schedule I or II), has currently accepted medical use in the United States, and may lead to moderate or low physical dependence or high psychological dependence.

SCHEDULE IV:

Substance has a low potential for abuse as compared to Schedule III, has currently accepted medical use in the United States, and abuse may lead to limited physical and psychological dependence

SCHEDULE V:

Substance has a low potential for abuse as compared to Schedule IV, has currently accepted medical use in the United States, and abuse has a narrow scope for physical and psychological dependence.

medicines that are Schedule III or higher (meaning they are less addictive than methadone) in order to treat opioid addiction. The only drug currently meeting this standard is buprenorphine, which is as effective as methadone for treating opioid addiction but is less addictive and safer to use. This means that physicians can help patients in their private offices, a desirable choice for some addicts who do not want to go to inpatient drug clinics. However, doctors do have to undergo special government-approved

When Chinese immigrants entered British Columbia they were viewed as a cheap source of labor for industry, but other Canadians viewed them as an economic threat. The first anti-drug legislation in Canada, the Opium Act of 1908, was in response to these anti-Chinese sentiments.

training, and there are limits on the number of patients one doctor can treat (30 as of 2005 legislation). Despite this, however, it is becoming easier for opioid-addicted persons to find treatment.

Canadian Drug Laws

Up until 1908, the use of opioids in Canada was unregulated. The use of alcohol and tobacco were considered more of a problem to public health and morals than opioids—but Chinese immigrants to Canada helped change the way Canadians felt about these drugs.

Early in the 1850s, Chinese immigrants began entering British Columbia in large numbers. Most did not have families to support and were able to work for low wages. They were considered a cheap source of labor for the railroads, mining, and other industries in western Canada. During this time period, the Chinese lived in communities that were relatively isolated, so the smoking of opium and the presence of opium dens were not considered harmful. At that time, the government's concerns over opium were more financial than anything else; it saw opium as a "cash cow" over which it didn't want to lose control. When British Columbia joined the confederation in 1871, the federal government placed a $500 licensing fee on Chinese opium factories.

During the 1880s, the Chinese began to be perceived as an "economic threat" to other Canadians. The decline of the railroads and the gold rush meant fewer employment opportunities overall. Canadians with families could not compete with the wages of unmarried Chinese laborers. As economic conditions deteriorated, the Chinese became a greater target for resentment and fear. Hostility toward the Chinese began to be reflected in Canadian legislation, which was designed to end Chinese immigration and drive the Chinese out of the economic mainstream in Canada. By 1904, the tax on Chinese immigrants had risen to $500 per person. While this seemed to slow Chinese immigration to Canada, Japanese immigration into British Colombia started to rise. This further fueled anti-Asiatic sentiments. After a major labor demonstration in 1907 (directed against Japanese immigrants), the Opium Act of 1908 was passed. This was Canada's first anti-drug legislation. The act made it an *indictable* offense to import, manufacture, offer to sell, sell, or possess to sell opium for nonmedical purposes, but did not prohibit simple possession or use.

Three years later, however, the 1908 Opium Act was repealed in favor of even harsher legislation. The 1908 Opium Act had created a black market for opium, and

There were two conflicting views on how to regard addiction in Canada, whether as a crime or as a disease. In the end, drugs were criminalized because of the widespread belief that drugs turned users into dangerous lunatics.

law enforcement interests believed that the way to stop the demand for opium was to create harsher penalties (including imprisonment) and to expand enforcement powers. The 1911 Act began the "enforcement" phase of Canadian drug policy, which continued unchallenged until the 1950s. Because few if any voices were speaking out for the treatment of drug users prior to the late 1950s, it was easy for enforcement-related interests to implement harsh anti-drug legislation. Imprisonment was a priority over treatment. In addition, because habitual drug use was associated mostly with Chinese immigrants, many Canadians felt they were immune from the effects of harsh drug legislation.

During the 1950s, despite the fact that illegal drug use was declining, the media published sensational accounts of drug addicted youth in Canada. During this period, the idea of treating habitual drug users was first considered a priority. Some physicians came to see drug addiction as their territory because it was beginning to be looked upon as a disease instead of a crime. These doctors believed that addiction should be regarded as a social and medical problem, not a criminal one. In response to the increased calls from the medical community for the treatment of drug users, the federal government established the Senate Special Committee on the Traffic of Narcotic Drugs in Canada in 1955. After holding hearings across the country, however, the committee ended up favoring the view of the law enforcement community. This perspective was eventually reflected in the harsh 1961 Narcotic Control Act.

The criminalization of drugs in Canada was made possible because of the strongly held belief that certain drugs had the ability to enslave users. By the 1960s and 1970s, these beliefs were being questioned again, however, and the emerging public health movement challenged the criminalization of drugs. The "dope fiend" mythology, which had been used for several decades to justify strict prohibition, became discredited because large numbers of middle-class youth were using illicit drugs recreationally without turning into dangerous lunatics. This narrowed the social distance between drug users and mainstream society; when a substantial proportion of the population is engaging in drug use, it is difficult to maintain myths that are not supported by experience. Canadian laws were criticized for making criminals out of white middle-class youth.

In 1969, the Commission of Inquiry into the Non Medical Use of Drugs (also known as the Le Dain Commission) studied the illicit drug issue in Canada. Between 1969 and 1973, the commission produced four reports. The most significant point in one of the reports was the

Heroin is classified in the United States as a Schedule I drug. Therefore, a first offense is considered a Class I felony and carries a minimum sentence of four to five months in prison.

recommendation to gradually withdraw the criminalization of illegal drugs.

In 1986, however, President Ronald Reagan declared a new war on drugs in the United States—and Canada followed suit. This began a new era of drug prohibition and law enforcement and led to the development of the Canadian Drug Strategy, which was first implemented in 1987. As part of the new drug strategy, a committee was formed to draft new legislation. Almost ten years later, in June of 1996, the Controlled Drugs and Substances Act (Bill C8) was voted into law. Although there is a strong voice in Canada for treating drug abuse as a disease rather than a crime, the ongoing policy remains based on a harsh system of law and punishment.

Punishments for Opioid Use

The punishment for opioid use varies depending on which schedule the drug falls under and how many times a user has been arrested. For Schedule I drugs, like heroin, even the first offense is considered a Class I felony. This means that in the United States, the minimum sentence is four to five months in prison. For the Schedule II drugs, like codeine and morphine, the first offense is a Class I misdemeanor. This carries a minimum sentence of forty-five days in jail, but no prison time. However, the second offense is considered a Class I felony, which again, carries with it a minimum sentence of four or five months in prison.

Clearly, opioid abuse can have serious consequences. For someone who has become addicted, however, treatment offers the only hope of escape from these far-reaching consequences.

6 Treatment

Doug grew up in the suburbs of London, England, in a stable family life in a middle-class neighborhood. He smoked his first marijuana reefer when he was fifteen, and from there he graduated to other "harder drugs" throughout his teen years.

I tried all the mainstream drugs in the following order: alcohol, cannabis, speed, LSD, Ecstasy, cocaine, ketamine, crack, and finally the big "H"— yes heroin. I had already discovered that I leaned towards the depressant drugs (except alcohol) and when I first "Chased the Dragon" (I have never injected and I never intend to), I had reached the pinnacle of pleasure. I have always loved cannabis and when I took the two together, I would drift for hours. The feeling is virtually indescribable, but the saying "wrapped up in cotton wool" sums it up. Any pain I have, be it physical or mental, just disappears, time doesn't seem to exist, and every so often I would realize just how detached from the "real" world I would be.

Doug's first relationship with heroin was pleasurable (apart from the nausea), but his source was unreliable, forcing him to go for days at a time without heroin. As a result, Doug did not consider himself addicted.

When Doug's girlfriend broke up with him, though, he turned to heroin to drown the pain. He began using

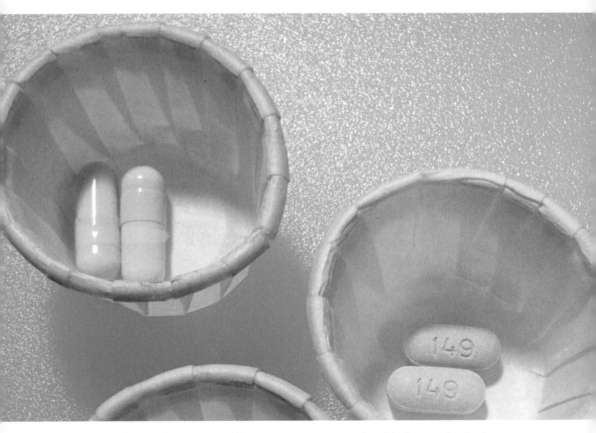

Morphine withdrawal symptoms are not just uncomfortable, but can be fatal. As a result, other drugs are administered that help wean the patient off the morphine.

it in the morning, during the day at work, and long into the night. He became so "wasted" that he couldn't even write properly, and eventually, he lost his job. Doug recalls, "I got in debt, lost loads of weight (I was skinny to begin with), and after seven months of hell, I finally went through *detox* with a case worker and two weeks' worth of drugs to counter the withdrawal symptoms—but not enough Valium, I can never have enough Valium. I finally got myself together, but only after a stint in a psychiatric ward—because after withdrawal, depression and boredom sets in."

Two years have gone by since Doug went through his first withdrawal, and now he is enrolled in yet another detox program. Doug says,

> The worrying thing is I have no reason to use again but without a shadow of a doubt I know I cannot handle heroin. The drug I am using to come off this time is Subutex (buprenorphine), and I must admit it is quite remarkable apart from the first day I took it. It puts me into withdrawal as the Subutex takes over the opioid receptor and gets rid of any other opioid already attached to it. The next day I felt totally fine, no cravings and no sickness. I take 8 milligrams a day but can easily get by on 4 milligrams. I don't get any real buzz from taking it, but then I am opioid dependant. It isn't absorbed into the bloodstream very well so I have to let the tablets dissolve under my tongue, which takes about fifteen minutes. . . . I have an addictive personality. Moderation and variety is the key; I will try and live by those words for the rest of my life.

Getting over a heroin addiction is a difficult process. Even the drugs that are used to help addicts recover are not without their dangers; many patients become addicted to the methadone used to wean them off morphine.

Doug's story, adapted from www.erowid.org/experiences/exp.php?ID=24623, shows how difficult the treatment process is for someone with heroin addiction. While there are many ways to detox from opioids, few of them work. Morphine addiction, one of the most common addictions to opioids, is extremely hard to cure. The withdrawal can kill an addict if he is not on other drugs to try to help cure him. Morphine withdrawal can lead to a stroke, heat attack, or even death. Because of this, a drug called methadone is often used to help wean a patient off the morphine. However, many times patients become addicted to the methadone instead.

In order to truly stop an addiction to morphine, one of the most proven methods is to be admitted into a rehabilitation center and then to go "cold turkey"—in other words, stop using any and all drugs at once. While this can be dangerous if a person tries it by herself, in a rehab center, staff take care of patients physically, while also providing a change of routine. (It is easier to end an addiction if behavior patterns don't stay the same.) Often, the best course of treatment is not simply drug therapy or simply behavioral therapy. A combination of the two should be used.

Methadone

Methadone is a medicine that is used for the treatment of opioid addiction. It works by occupying the opioid receptors in the brain instead of the abused opioid. This allows the person to stop using the drug without going through withdrawal. The drug is taken orally once a day, and works to suppress withdrawal symptoms for twenty-four to thirty-six hours. It blocks the high from the opioids, yet provides the body with the drug that it has come to depend on. However, it does not actually end an addiction; a user is still physically dependant on opioids. All methadone does is keep an addict from feeling withdrawal symptoms, as well as stopping the extreme mood swings that many addicts have as the level of opioids in their blood rises and falls. Because it does not end the user's need for an opioid in his body, methadone is often addictive in itself and is considered a Schedule II drug. However, it's seen as a better addiction to have; methadone is safer for the patient than many opioids are when taken regularly.

It has been thoroughly studied so that it can be used safely, allowing those in treatment to enter (or reenter) the workforce and establish a social and family life beyond the community of drug abusers. Methadone is also a cheaper alternative to prison time, which would cost thousands of dollars in tax money. Methadone can also stop the spread of HIV/AIDS, as well as other diseases that are spread by sharing needles.

Methadone is longer lasting than many other opioids, mostly because of its high *solubility* in the body's fat. The drug has a half-life of twenty-four to forty-eight hours, meaning that it can be taken once a day and still provide relief from withdrawal symptoms.

The History of Methadone

Max Bockmühl and Gustav Ehrhart in Germany first discovered methadone, a synthetic chemical, in 1937. They were looking for a painkiller that would be easier to use in surgery and have a low addiction potential. In 1947, the chemical giant Eli Lilly and Company introduced the drug to the United States. It quickly became used both as a low-price alternative for treating narcotic addiction and for pain management. Methadone was sold under the

One rumor claims that the name Dolophine was not coined because of its Latin roots, but instead was a tribute to Adolph Hitler and that the drug name was originally spelled "adolphine." While this has been proven to be false, it is still considered a fact by Scientologists. When Tom Cruise, a popular actor and member of the Church of Scientology, pointed this out in an interview with Entertainment Weekly, the magazine replied by pointing out the fact that the name was created after World War II by an American company who had no desire or motivation for naming a drug after Hitler.

Methadone works for the treatment of heroin addiction because it occupies the opioid receptors in the brain. This prevents the user from experiencing withdrawal symptoms, but does not remove the user's dependence on opioids.

name Dolophine®, which derives from the Latin words meaning "pain" and "end."

Buprenorphine

Buprenorphine is another drug that is used to combat opioid addiction. It was first approved by the U.S. Food and Drug Administration (FDA) in 2002 and is prescribed both alone, in the drug Subutex®, and in combination with naloxone in Suboxone®. The combination drug was designed to reduce bubrenorphine's potential to be abused by injection. These two drugs are the only Schedule III drugs that are used to combat opioid addiction; there are no Schedule IV or V opioids approved for treating opioid addiction. Schedule III classification means that they have a legitimate medical purpose, a lower chance for abuse, and are generally safer than schedule II drugs.

Buprenorphine is what is referred to as an opioid partial agonist. This means that it is an opioid and produces similar effects to other opioids, even the euphoria and respiratory depression. However, it works on a much smaller scale than opioids like opium and heroin do. Because its effects are smaller and less noticeable, the drug is used only to help addicts stop using other opioids and does not have as great a potential for abuse itself. There are some side effects to buprenorphine, many of which are the same as other opioids. Nausea, vomiting, and constipation are all problems.

EFFECTIVENESS OF TREATMENT METHODS FOR OPIOID ADDICTION

	Buprenorphine n=55	High Dose Methadone n=55	Low-Dose Methadone n=55
Average # of days that patients remained in treatment	96	105	70
Patients with 12 or more consecutive drug-free urine samples	26%	28%	8%

Table modified from http://www.drugabuse.gov/NIDA_Notes/NNVol16N2/Buprenorphine.html

Buprenorphine has proven to be an effective treatment for opioid addiction. This table shows that it is more effective that the low dose methadone treatment, and works faster than the high dose methadone treatment.

Brand Name vs. Generic Name

Talking about medications can be confusing because every drug has at least two names: its "generic name" and the "brand name" that the pharmaceutical company uses to market the drug. Generic names are based on the drug's chemical structure, while drug companies use brand names in order to inspire public recognition and loyalty for their products.

Drug Approval

Before a drug can be marketed in the United States, it must be officially approved by the Food and Drug Administration (FDA). Today's FDA is the primary consumer protection agency in the United States. Operating under the authority given it by the government, and guided by laws established throughout the twentieth century, the FDA has established a rigorous drug approval process that verifies the safety, effectiveness, and accuracy of labeling for any drug marketed in the United States.

While the United States has the FDA for the approval and regulation of drugs and medical devices, Canada has a similar organization called the Therapeutic Product Directorate (TPD). The TPD is a division of Health Canada, the Canadian government's department of health. The TPD regulates drugs, medical devices, disinfectants, and sanitizers with disinfectant claims. Some of the things that the TPD monitors are quality, effectiveness, and safety. Just as the FDA must approve new drugs in the United States, the TPD must approve new drugs in Canada before those drugs can enter the market.

The clinical treatment of addicts with buprenorphine has three phases. The first is called the induction phase, where a user who has abstained from opioids for at least twenty-four hours (and is therefore in the early stages of withdrawal) is given buprenorphine. This stage is medically monitored; if the patient has other opioids in her system, the buprenorphine could make the body go into

It seems wrong that such a lovely flower should be the source of problems for so many people. Opioid addiction is terrible, but treatment offers hope to prisoners of this perilous plant.

114 Chapter 6—Treatment

acute withdrawal. The second stage is the stabilization phase, when a patient no longer has cravings for the opioid. Due to the chance of side effects, the dosage of buprenorphine is often adjusted at this stage. The third and final stage is the maintenance phase, when the patient has responded well to a set dosage of the drug. Once a user is not dependant on the original opioid, there are two choices: to keep a patient on the buprenorphine indefinitely as long as she continues to do well on the drug—or to stop the drug gradually and put the patient through a medically supervised withdrawal. While the symptoms in the second scenario will not be as severe as they would have been if the opioids were still in the bloodstream, they will last longer.

Heroin and other opioids can wreak havoc on a person's life, causing serious social, physical, and legal problems. Addiction has the potential to be lethal—but treatment offers real hope. Although recovery is difficult, it is possible.

Glossary

abatement: Reducing, ending, or suppressing something.

ampules: Small, sealed glass containers that hold a measured amount of a medicinal substance to be injected.

anorexia: An eating disorder characterized by excessive dieting to the point of serious ill-health and sometimes death.

black market: A system of buying and selling officially controlled goods illegally.

Canary wine: A sweet, white wine from the Canary Islands.

cede: To surrender something to another power.

condiment: A substance added to food to improve or adjust its flavor.

contracted: Caught an illness or disease.

cortisol: A steroid hormone secreted by the adrenal glands in response to inflammation caused by tissue damage; also called hydrocortisone.

detox: Detoxification; to rid the body of toxins.

endocrine system: The glands that secrete hormones internally directly into the lymphatic system or bloodstream.

endorphins: Substances in the brain that attach to the same cell receptors that morphine does.

euphoric: Feeling intense joy or happiness.

frogspawn: A floating mass of fertilized frog's eggs protected in a jelly-like substance.

half-life: The time it takes for half a given amount of a substance such as a drug to be removed from living tissue through natural biological activity.

hypothalamus: A central area on the underside of the brain, controlling involuntary functions such as body temperature.

indictable: Liable to being charged with a criminal offense.

infectious: Used to describe a disease that can be passed from one person to another.

isolationism: A government policy based on the belief that national interests are best served by avoiding economic and political alliances with other countries.

Kaposi's sarcoma: A cancer of connective tissue that causes purplish-red patches on the skin.

lethargy: A state of physical slowness and mental dullness as a result of tiredness, disease, or drugs.

lymphoma: A malignant tumor originating in a lymph node.

mandated: Ordered.

opportunistic: Used to describe a microorganism or minor disease that is not normally serious but that can become life threatening when the host has a weakened immune system.

pathogen: Something that can cause a disease.

peristalsis: The involuntary muscle contractions that transport food, waste, or other contents through a tube-shaped organ such as the intestine.

pictograms: Graphic symbols or pictures representing a word or idea.

pneumocystis carinii pneumonia: A form of pneumonia that mainly affects people with weakened immune systems.

pulmonary edema: An abnormal buildup of fluid in the lungs.

quinine: A bitter-tasting drug made from cinchona bark, used to treat some forms of malaria.

reparations: Compensation demanded of a defeated nation by the victor in a war.

Ritalin: Trademark for methylphenidate, a drug used to treat attention-deficit/hyperactivity disorder.

sedatives: Drugs that produce a calming effect.

seizures: Convulsions, sensory disturbances, or loss of consciousness, resulting from abnormal electrical discharges in the brain (as in epilepsy).

SIDS (sudden infant death syndrome): The clinical name for crib death, the sudden, unexplained death of a small baby while sleeping.

solubility: The extent to which one substance is able to dissolve in another.

spontaneous abortions: Miscarriages.

stereotypes: Oversimplified ideas held by one person or group about another, usually based on incomplete or inaccurate information.

stillbirths: The birth of a dead fetus after the twenty-eighth week of pregnancy.

synthetic: Made artificially by a chemical process of synthesis so as to resemble a natural product.

testosterone: A male steroid hormone produced in the testicles and responsible for the development of secondary sex characteristics.

tinctures: A solution of a plant product or chemical substance in alcohol.

toxoplasmosis: A disease of mammals caused by a toxoplasma transmitted to humans via undercooked meat of through contact with infectious animals, especially cats.

tuberculosis: A highly infectious disease that affects the lungs.

Further Reading

Davenport-Hines, Richard. *The Pursuit of Oblivion: A Global History of Narcotics.* New York: Norton, 2002.

Esherick, Joan. *Dying for Acceptance. A Teen's Guide to Drug and Alcohol-Related Health Issues.* Broomall, Pa.: Mason Crest, 2005.

Harris, Nancy (ed.). *Opioids.* Farmington Hills, Mich.: Thomson Gale, 2005.

Lawton, Sandra Augustyn (ed.). *Drug Information for Teens: Health Tips About the Physical and Mental Effects of Substance Abuse: Including Information About Marijuana, Inhalants, Club Drugs, Stimulants, Hallucinogens, Opioids, Prescription and Over-the-Counter Drugs.* Detroit, Mich.: Omnigraphics, 2006.

Libal, Joyce. *Substance Related Disorders and Their Treatment.* Broomall, Pa.: Mason Crest, 2004.

Pinsky, Drew, Stephanie Brown, Robert J. Meyers, and William White. *When Painkillers Become Dangerous: What Everyone Needs to Know About OxyContin and Other Prescription Drugs.* Center City, Minn.: Hazelden Publishing, 2004.

Walker, Ida. *Painkillers: Prescription Dependency.* Broomall, Pa.: Mason Crest, 2008.

For More Information

American Pain Society
www.ampainsoc.org

American Society of Addiction Medicine
www.asam.org

Center for Drug Evaluation and Information
www.fda.gov/cder/drug/infopage/oxycontin

National Institute on Drug Abuse
www.nida.nih.gov

Parenting Teens
www.parentingteens.com/prescription_drug_abuse.html

Teens Health
kidshealth.org/teen/drug_alcohol/drugs/prescription_drug_abuse.
html

Waismann Method Advanced Treatment of Opioid Dependency
www.opioids.com

World Health Organization
www.who.int

The websites listed on this page were active at the time of publication. The publisher is not responsible for websites that have changed their addresses or discontinued operation since the date of publication. The publisher will review and update the website list upon each reprint.

Bibliography

Drugstory.org. "Chasing the High—An Interview with Josh." http://www.drugstory.org/feature/josh.asp.

Erowid Experience Vaults. "Climbing the Experience Ladder." http://www.erowid.org/experiences/exp.php?ID=24623.

Jean Tweed Center. "Opioids." http://www.jeantweed.com/opioids.htm.

Kouri, Jim. "Women Abusing Opioids at Higher Rate Than Men." http://www.theconservativevoice.com/article/15575.html.

LSUHSC Worksite Health Services. "Facts About Drugs: Opioids." http://www.lsuhsc.edu/no/organizations/CampusHealth/brochures/opioids.pdf.

Narcanon California. "Drug Information: Morphine." http://www.narconon.ca/morphine.htm.

Narcanon California. "The History of Opium." http://www.stopopiateabuse.com/history-of-opioids.htm.

Narcanon California. "Opium." http://www.narconon.ca/opium.htm.

National Institute on Drug Abuse. "As a Matter of Fact . . . Heroin and Other Opioids." http://www.well.com/user/woa/fsheroin.htm.

National Institute on Drug Abuse. "NIDA InfoFacts: Heroin." http://www.nida.nih.gov/Infofacts/heroin.html.

National Institute on Drug Abuse. "Research Report Series—Heroin Abuse and Addiction." http://www.drugabuse.gov/ResearchReports/Heroin/heroin2.html#scope.

Office of National Drug Control Policy. "Drug Facts: Heroin." http://www.whitehousedrugpolicy.gov/drugfact/heroin/index.html.

Office of National Drug Control Policy. "Methadone April 2000." http://www.whitehousedrugpolicy.gov/publications/factsht/methadone/index.html.

"The Opioids." http://www.drugtext.org/sub/opiat1.html.

"Opioids." http://www.sayno.com/opioids.html.

Osler, William. "The Plant of Joy." http://www.opioids.net.

Schaffer Library of Drug Policy. "Morphine." http://www.druglibrary. org/SCHAFFER/heroin/opifaq.htm#Morphine.

Schaffer Library of Drug Policy. "The Opioids." http://www. druglibrary.org/schaffer/heroin/opioids.htm.

U.S. Department of Health and Human Services, Substance Abuse and Mental Health Services Administration, Center for Substance Abuse Treatment. "Buprenorphine." http://buprenorphine.samhsa. gov/about.html.

The Vaults of Erowid. "Heroin." http://www.erowid.org/chemicals/ heroin/heroin.shtml.

Index

addiction 12, 16, 24, 37, 46, 51, 57, 60, 81, 83, 87, 93, 96, 100, 101, 108, 109, 111, 112, 115
Afghanistan 16, 92
Ambien 10
apomorphine 23
Arabia 33

Baum, L. Frank 12
Bayer 46
black tar heroin 15
Bockmuhl, Max 110
Britain 27, 28, 41, 42, 44
buprenorphine 107, 111, 112, 113, 115
Burma 16, 92
Burton, Robert 38

Canada 19, 25, 92, 96, 98, 99, 100, 101, 102, 103, 113
China 27, 28, 29, 30, 34, 35, 42, 44, 45
Civil War 40, 41
cocaine 17, 49, 70, 71, 89, 95, 105
codeine 15, 17, 18, 19, 24, 41, 51, 54, 57, 96, 103
Coricidin 10
cortisol 23, 116

depression 53, 71, 107
Dolophine 110, 111
dross 35
drug laws 94–99
drug schedules 96, 102, 103, 109, 112
Dutch 34, 37

Egypt 33
Ehrhart, Gustav 110
Eli Lilly 111
Emperor Tao Kwang 27, 29, 42
endocrine system 23, 73, 116
endorphin receptors 21, 23
endorphins 21
England 30, 42, 51, 105

fentanyl 19, 24
Food and Drug Administration (FDA) 111, 113

Germany 49, 110
Greece 16, 33, 34

Harrison Narcotics Act 49, 95
hepatitis 74–76
heroin
    abuse of 15
    effects of 9
    street names 15
HIV/AIDS 11, 16, 71, 74, 76, 110
Hong Kong 42
hul gil 33
hydrocodone 19, 24, 51, 57, 96
Hypnos 34
hypodermic needle 16, 17, 41, 73
hypothalamus 23, 117

immigrants 46, 96, 98, 99
India 34
International Opium Conference 46

laudanum 35, 38, 39
liver disease 74–76

marijuana 63, 71, 105
meperidine 19, 24
Mesopotamia 33
methadone 19, 24, 92, 108, 109, 110, 111, 112
methamphetamine 17
Morpheus 16
morphine
    abuse of 41, 51, 53, 95–96, 103
    as painkiller 16–17
    discovery of 16, 38–41
    effects of 21, 68
    use during Civil War 41
    withdrawal 108–109
Muslims 33

naloxone 111
narcotics 20, 21, 22, 49, 95, 96

"on the nod" 21
opioids
     abuse of 52–53
     as anesthesia 57
     as medicines 37–49, 54
     effects of 20, 21, 63–74
     source of 12, 13, 14
     synthetic 14
     types of 15–19
opium
     abuse of 16, 17, 27
     history of 27–38
opium dens 34, 35, 95, 98
opium pipes 34, 35
opium wars 28, 30, 42
overdose 84–87
oxycodone 18, 19, 24
OxyContin 10

painkillers 10, 19, 22, 25, 37, 41
Paracelsus 38, 39
Paracodol 54
patent medicines 36, 37, 41
Paveral 19
Percocet 9, 10, 18
Percodan 18
Persia 33, 46
poppy
     flower 13, 14, 15, 16, 19, 30, 33, 34, 35, 41, 45, 46
     oil 31, 33, 45
     seeds 14, 31, 33, 45
prescription drugs 9, 10, 11, 25, 54
prison 11, 12, 61, 91, 92, 93, 94, 95, 102, 103, 110
propoxyphene 19, 24

Queen Victoria 27, 42
quinine 16

respiratory depression 71–73
Robiquet, Pierre-Jean 41

Sears Roebuck 41
sedatives 20, 22, 118
Sertürner, Friedrich Wilhelm Adam 16, 38, 40

"soldier's disease" 40, 41
Somnos 34
Suboxone 111
Subutex 107, 111
Sydenham, Thomas 38

testosterone 23
tetanus 76
Therapeutic Product Directorate (TPD) 113
tolerance 16, 20, 38, 57, 73, 81, 84
treatment 11, 96, 99, 101, 103, 108, 109, 111, 112, 113, 115
Treaty of Nanjing 42, 44
Treaty of Tientsin 44
Tse-hsu, Lin 27, 42
Tylenol 18, 54
Tylox 18

U.N. Commission of Narcotic Drugs 49
Unisom 10
United Nations 49
United States 15, 19, 35, 45, 46, 49, 57, 59, 61, 78, 92, 94, 102, 103, 111, 113

Vicodin 10

The Wizard of Oz 12, 13, 14
World War I 49
World War II 49, 110
Wright, C.R. Alder 46

Picture Credits

Brand X Pictures
Colin Anderson 82, 111
    Steve Allen 72
Comstock Images 10, 106
Corbis 60, 85, 88, 93, 94, 102
Drug Enforcement Agency 65, 70
istock.com 18, 31, 40, 98, 114
    FhF Greenmedia 31, 114
    José Carlos Pires Pereira 40
    Mary Marin 98
    Olga Zorina 18
Jupiter Images 8, 14,17, 22, 28, 32, 35, 39, 44, 50, 52, 56, 69, 78, 86, 90, 104
Library of Congress 36, 43
National Institutes of Health 80, 112
PhotoAlto 108
Photodisc 74
Robertson, D. Gordon E. 100
Sebastian Kaulitzki 77
Stockbyte 48, 55, 66, 97

To the best knowledge of the publisher, all other images are in the public domain. If any image has been inadvertently uncredited, please notify Harding House Publishing Services, Vestal, New York 13850, so that rectification can be made for future printings.

Author and Consultant Biographies

Author

In addition to being an author and journalist, E. J. Sanna has a background in chemistry. She also enjoys traveling, music, and theater.

Series Consultant

Jack E. Henningfield, Ph.D., is a professor at the Johns Hopkins University School of Medicine, and he is also Vice President for Research and Health Policy at Pinney Associates, a consulting firm in Bethesda, Maryland, that specializes in science policy and regulatory issues concerning public health, medications development, and behavior-focused disease management. Dr. Henningfield has contributed information relating to addiction to numerous reports of the U.S. Surgeon General, the National Academy of Sciences, and the World Health Organization.